EXCERPTS FROM AN AFRICAN DIARY

PAULA DRAYCON

Published by

MELROSE BOOKS

An Imprint of Melrose Press Limited
St Thomas Place, Ely
Cambridgeshire
CB7 4GG, UK
www.melrosebooks.com

FIRST EDITION

Cover designed by Jeremy Kay

ISBN 978 1 907040 29 0

Printed and bound in Great Britain by:
CLE Digital Solutions. St Ives, Cambridgeshire

FSC
Mixed Sources
Product group from well-managed
forests and other controlled sources

Cert no. TT-COC-003115
www.fsc.org
© 1996 Forest Stewardship Council

DEDICATION

I DEDICATE THIS BOOK TO MY THREE EXTRAORDINARY friends, Carolyn in England, Mary in New Zealand, the late Marie Petit in South Africa, and to my sister Fiona in England.

It is because of their significant and diverse influence and their unwavering faith in me that I am the person I am today. They have always supported my beliefs, encouraged my dreams and provided me with homes around the world.

Without the loving home that my mother and late father provided and the wonderful holidays in the English countryside we as a family spent together my journey through life could well have been very different.

My spiritual wealth has also played a pivotal role in my lifestyle, and I can only be thankful for the opportunities I have had, and the strength with which I have been able to respond to them.

To all the many people around the world who have played a 'meaningful' part in my life – I acknowledge and thank you here.

As you read this book, you will recognize a little part of yourself.

The long periods between the journal entries were due to the years spent working and travelling in England and New Zealand.

ACKNOWLEDGEMENTS

T HE LATE DAME MURIEL POWELL, MATRON OF the St George's group of hospitals London (1947-1969) for her ethical approach to life, which rubbed off on me.

Carolyn Loughborough (nee Ellis), my best friend and close nursing colleague in the late 1960s and early 1970s. You instilled a confidence in me, second to none.

Mary O'Neill. My dear Kiwi friend and spiritual mentor. You and your family welcomed me into your humble home in New Zealand in 1972. It was from this large family that I learned so much about life itself. Aroha Nui Mary.

Margaret Darby, in New Zealand, and the late Lucia Birkenstock in South Africa. Both matrons in their respective hospitals across the globe. They continually re-employed me during my years of travelling between the two countries.

My nursing colleagues around the world, who have toiled tirelessly around the clock to serve others; some of you have waited patiently for this book.

Peter, John and Fiona, my brothers and sister, who have never fully understood why I chose to live in Africa, but who have always welcomed me home to England.

Simon, my nephew and Godson, who understands everything. Thank you for believing in me and my cause.

Oscar, my great nephew, and Caitlin my great niece, in whom I place my faith. I cherish the thought that you can make a difference for your generation, and that you will come to know of the joys and rich blessings that Africa imparts.

Virginia McKenna. You trusted me enough to share a little of your life with me, and you were able to discern the depth of my feelings for Africa. Thank you for facilitating the fruition of this forty-five year old dream and for the honour of being referred to as 'a kindred spirit'. My grateful thanks for your support whilst I continued to write this book, and especially for compiling the foreword. xx

The late Marie Petit. My beloved friend in Africa, without whom none of this would have happened. You drove the kombi over hundreds of thousands of kilometres in southern Africa, enabling me to photograph and document a disappearing world. Right from the start you said "you should write a book."

Melrose Books who gave me the break I had longed for.

Kay and Richard Carr. You have been there for me every step of the way since Marie's death. Your love, support and motivation 'to get back into the writer's seat' has been uplifting. *'We won't forget anything, will we?'* xx

Thank you so much Oriah; not only for allowing me to use your poem in my book, but also for the 'know how' Gratitude also for the blessings; they are very important! I know how busy you must be, so am really grateful. African blessings from Nkulunkulu to you. Paula

CONTENTS

FOREWORD

Joy Adamson often used to talk about 'The spirit of Elsa'. An invisible thread of understanding and compassion that weaves itself around us and unites friends and strangers alike. As it will surely bind all of us who read this book. This unusual book. It is a slight book, but a deep book. A book with a soul. Not only of the writer but of Africa. Africa illuminates and throbs and pulses on every page and enlivens every step taken by Paula Draycon on her voyage of discovery during more than thirty years. And her discovery also, is twofold. It is of Africa and Paula herself.

In a very personal way, she takes us with her on her journey and we will become willing companions as we enter into her world, with her perspective, her way of looking at things.

Those of us who have travelled in Africa will identify with her wonder at the beauty of nature – whether harsh or exotic. Will grieve with her on her visit in 2006 to a ravaged Zimbabwe, at the senseless killing of a baboon in Kruger, at the mutilated carcass of an elephant slaughtered by the trophy and ivory poachers.

But such dark images are only a part of Paula's story. Fascinated by all the creatures that live in the bush, her vivid descriptions of bird life, riverbanks, insects and plants reveal, to me, the essence of who she is. Perhaps her training as a nurse when she was young, her transition from nurse to a teacher of nurses, her deep religious faith – all played their part.

It is impossible not to be moved by her joyous feelings of 'homecoming' when she sets off on one of her safaris. The blue flash of a kingfisher, a feather on the wind, walking in silence where the Bushmen used to tread – and her memorable pilgrimage to Elsa's grave. Whether in prose, verse or through quotations, Paula's stories and observations encourage us to stop and look, stop and listen, pause and wonder at nature. Red in tooth and claw sometimes, it is true, but overwhelming in its beauty and mystery.

Elsa's spirit has moved its magic once more.

Virginia McKenna

INTRODUCTION
THE SEEDS

GROWING UP IN ENGLAND IS WHAT MOST English children do. Although unaware at the time, I can now empathise with the words of Kuki Gallman in Kenya, *"You can't choose where you are born, but you can choose where you live and die."*

Upon my imaginary horse, I rode the hills that kissed the boundaries of my home in Yorkshire, enabling me to combine my love of adventure with the natural environment. Whilst riding my four-legged friend I met a few other wild horses, but at some stage I must have met God, and, as far as I remember, I didn't tell anyone!

It wasn't long before I rode out with the specific intention of 'meeting God'; He wasn't hard to find, because He seemed to be everywhere, and yet, not many of my friends had mentioned Him. This then, became my first recollection of my own conscience; should I introduce Him to others, or keep Him to myself?

My father seemed to foster such aspirations for me, and as each of my birthdays passed I perceived his dreams for me with increased vitality. My father was probably my first mentor and role model.

He taught me to have faith in myself.

He taught me to dream.

He taught me about honesty and integrity.

He taught me to try, try, and if all else failed to try again.

He taught me to love the outdoors, and to respect all forms of life.

He taught me about the value of self-criticism and reflection.

He taught me about the benefits of self-reliance, and that by spending time alone, the discovery of self was priceless.

Although he didn't teach me about God, I found God at a young age through his teachings. It just happened to be on my horse.

Toni, my mother, was the epitome of a nurturing carer. She played the piano, and in the English winters the family gathered around her to sing. I was indeed my father's daughter, and soon relished 'going solo'. One of my favourite songs was Shirley Temple's 'Animal Crackers'.

It is from the safekeeping of my memory that I am fortunate enough to possess the ability to recall so many people and places that have helped to mould my life and my motivation for living.

It is important that these memories are not forgotten. A memory can fade but, eventually, it will die along with its owner. The failure to transmit a communication could result in the permanent loss of valuable information, some of which originates from our ancestral roots.

My mother was my second mentor and guiding force. She taught me the benefits of good hygiene, nutrition and a glowing appearance.

She taught me to be practical and organised.

She taught me the benefits of attending Sunday School where I would learn that "Jesus wanted me for a sunbeam."

She taught me to sing and to enjoy music.

She taught me the merits of team games.

She taught me not to blame myself if things didn't pan out.

She taught me to lean on others a little.

She taught me to break with tradition occasionally, in order to be noticed.

In the summer months, my parents would take us for picnics at the coast. En route, we would pass by poppy fields, vivid patches of red amidst the green countryside. I can still hear my mother exclaiming, "Look at the poppies, we are nearly there!" I loved adventure, even then. I thrived on the expectancy of being 'nearly there'; unknowingly, my lust for discovery was in its infancy. By enjoying the journey, the joy of reaching the destination was doubled.

Fortunately, school was a place I valued. I remain indebted to the educators who facilitated my intellectual growth. I particularly remember the nature study classes whilst I was still in primary school. Split into small groups, and holding each other's hands, our teacher would lead us into the countryside. Our respect for the flowers and trees, the insects, birds and animals came naturally. Our teacher had an almost reverent regard for all living things. She showed us rosehips, pussy willow and cuckoo spit. We loved to hear the cuckoo calling. It was, then, a common sound. Quite naturally, I found a strong attachment to the study of nature and can relate the origin of my inquisitiveness about life and its purpose to these years. It was in surroundings such as these where I found solace.

One day, two-year-old Jeremy came to live with us. Jeremy, a fluffy abandoned Pomeranian, became my shadow. I had never known such love for another living creature, and I now realise that my happiest and 'warmest' moments were when I was either with Jeremy or when I indulged my imagination by infusing my soul with dreams of faraway places.

Life without Jeremy could have been intolerable at times, and I owe so much to him. We became partners and he pulled me through some of my darkest hours as a growing teenager.

It was in the early 1960s that I recall another powerful influence in my life. The story of Elsa the lioness was emerging. Elsa, an orphaned cub, was reared and subsequently released back into the wild, in Africa, by George and Joy Adamson.

Born Free was the title of Joy's book. It was the true and poignant account of a lion cub orphaned by the bullets from the rifles of George Adamson and Ken Smith; bullets which killed the mother of three cubs in the Northern Frontier district of Kenya. George had been ordered to seek out and dispose of a lion, reportedly a man-eater. When he and Ken were charged by a lioness shots were fired. Only on inspection of the corpse was the reason for her charge made clear. This was not the reported man-eater, but a lioness with swollen teats, protecting her young litter.

Born Free was a truly authentic African story. It told of the joys and the sorrows of the Adamsons' friendship with a lioness. A lioness who was equally happy with her human foster parents as she was with her wild mate and father to her cubs.

At a young age, I had read the book and watched the movie which appeared annually on British TV screens. I recall being moved beyond belief by the Academy Award-winning movie. Virginia McKenna and her husband Bill Travers played the star roles of Joy and George Adamson.

Never in my short lifetime had a story evoked such emotion in me, nor stirred such a deep-rooted longing to journey toward the cradle of mankind. The sadness, yet the magnitude of this epic, along with its own tale of courage and love, fashioned my dreams.

A teenager living in England realised that life offered so much, and she was about to commence an incredible journey. Slowly and sometimes unknowingly, it became her driving force, as the first seeds of Africa were being blown into her very being.

One day I would go to Africa, and walk in the footsteps of Elsa and the Adamsons.

During, and following, completion of my nursing training in 1970 lions and Africa were temporarily erased from the forefront of my mind. In 1972 my travelling career started and I was on my way to New Zealand by ship. However, I was not meant to forget Africa for long. The second port of call on the voyage to New Zealand was Cape Town. Arriving at sunrise, with Table Mountain as a backdrop, the seeds in my soul took root. Something happened, an instinct stirred – and I was drawn towards the mountain.

Eight hours in dock was just enough time. At the top of the mountain there was a three hundred and sixty degree view of Africa – to the north a hinterland, a spiritual magnet pulling me towards it. The strength required to leave the mountain and resume my journey to New Zealand was immense.

Four years later, and casting aside any obstacles, my plan was in place. In early 1976 I stepped back onto African soil. It seemed so right.

A year's nursing contract at St Augustine's Hospital in Durban afforded me the opportunities to pursue my inherent desire to seek out the challenge and the solace of the wild areas and game reserves of southern Africa. All previous love affairs paled in comparison to the deep relationship I formed with the big heart of Africa.

Due to many and varied commitments this love affair of note involved twelve years of episodic departures from and arrivals in Africa. These phases allowed me the grace to live the quintessential lifestyle of Africa, at the same time bonding with its ancestral inheritance. During these times, I was also allowed long periods of reflection from outside of the African continent, during which time my life's philosophy and deeply rooted feelings were nurtured. My love of photography and storytelling was enhanced; indeed, the magnetism of Africa had cast its spell on me.

Closing in on my fortieth birthday I finally realised my destiny. I was to live permanently in Africa. I purchased my first puppy, a Rhodesian Ridgeback (commonly known as the lion dog), and predictably named her Elsa. Only at this stage did I become vaguely aware that I was following a passage mapped by someone or something far greater than I could imagine.

In 1993, and following as much time as I was able to spend in the game reserves of southern Africa, I experienced a profound revelation. An intensely secretive, timid and very beautiful bird, clothed in feathers of bright red, purple and emerald green, flew to within metres of where I was sitting in my garden. It was a purple-crested loerie.

Perhaps on that particular day I was more open to that mystical space where the soul is finely divided from the spirit, a place where secret emotions and thoughts are revealed to one's cognisant mind. I reflected on the coincidence of both of my guardian angels, in New Zealand and in South Africa, being of the same faith. Later in the day, I contacted the local Catholic priest, and discussed the possibility of my conversion into the devotion of Roman Catholicism.

Only after my acceptance into the faith did I realise that the colours of the priest's vestments, depending on the liturgical season, are bright red, purple and emerald green. As I became more open to the depth and the relevance of my chosen spiritual path, I became aware that perhaps there was significance to the purpose in my life.

My faith has subsequently endowed me with considerable depth to my life.

During the late 1990s I found my thoughts diverting more frequently to the *Born Free* movie and the life of Elsa and her cubs. I had seen the movie, and viewed the documentaries of the lives of the Adamsons. I had read the biographies and the autobiographies. I had pondered over the Adamsons' accounts of life and death in the Kenyan bush. I had spent many moments of my life reflecting on photographs of Elsa's life, right up until her untimely death. For me, her grave became sacrosanct. I became almost an expert on the subject of Elsa's life and death. I was convinced that Elsa's spirit was responsible for my sublime happiness in life.

Quote:

In the beginnings of all things, wisdom and knowledge were with the animals, because Tirawa, the one above, did not speak directly to man. He sent certain animals to tell man that he showed himself through the beasts. Only from them and from the stars and the sun and the moon should man learn… all things tell of Tirawa.

Eagle Chief, Pawnee Tribe. From Native American Wisdom.

Knowing the remoteness of Elsa's Camp in the Meru reserve I realised that the possibility of my being able to touch the grave and thank Elsa's spirit, in the land of her birth, was also remote. Elsa's guidance transcended the life I had been born into, and my need to kneel at her grave was paramount.

Around the year 2000, two miracles happened. Firstly, and at a time when I felt the necessity to share, and in fact bequeath my lifetime's knowledge and experience of nursing to others, my career path changed. I was appointed to a position of teaching and facilitating student nurses. I regarded this to be a very noble charge. Secondly, I learned that a luxury lodge had been developed on Mugwongo Hill in the Meru National Park, Kenya. Its name was Elsa's Kopje. My heart was set.

At the beginning of a new millennium, I was the happiest person alive. Student nurses need happy stories, they need motivation, and they need to know that objectives can be achieved. At this time stories of Elsa and her cubs were told and received with delight and meaning within the hospital's clinical teaching laboratory

In the interim, my Ridgeback, Elsa, died. I cannot talk about this. However, my next two puppies were named after Elsa's wild cubs. Jespah, a Labrador, and Gopa, a Rhodesian Ridgeback. They had the freedom of my large African home and as predicted I loved them.

In May 2003, and throwing caution and finances to the wind, I made the decision to make a solo journey to a place about which I had first dreamed in the 1960s.

Once in Meru I could feel the presence of Elsa the lioness, the Adamsons, and indeed, Elsa, my very special dog, the ones who had influenced my life from those early days up to the present.

Following my uniquely meaningful experience in Meru I pursued my dream further, which led me into another dimension altogether. I met Virginia at her home in Surrey. We became kindred spirits, and subsequently, a sincere and gracious friendship evolved.

Nothing could have prepared me for what was to follow.

Quote:
There are no accidents. Those who are meant to meet, will meet. They are ready for each other.

Unknown

PREFACE

M Y LOVE FOR THE AFRICAN WILDERNESS AND the desire to seek out the last refuge of its wildlife has, for as long as I can remember, been paramount. It is in the quiet corners of the secluded touchstones of Africa's diverse landscapes that I have always found solace and ethereal wellbeing, and I can recall that from a tender age I wanted to experience and be part of that humbling environment, where mundane materialism has no place.

I felt it my right to search for a heritage before it disappeared like a vacuum, sucked into the clutches of man's greed and ignorance.

For many years, these physically concealed, yet spiritually liberating places were my church, because it was here, whilst engulfed by the starkness of the quiet beauty, that I became more aware of creation than anywhere else in the world that I had been. And I felt privileged to have known *life*, in the true sense of the word.

My travels through southern Africa and the sojourns I enjoyed furnished me with a sympathetic awareness and understanding of the needs and rights to which every living creature is entitled, and the role that they play in the ecological jigsaw of our planet. If one piece is lost, the damage is irreparable and the eye sees only the space which human carelessness has inflicted.

I grew increasingly at ease with the rhapsody of nature and its myriad of life forms, and my ability to philosophise in the stillness grew with my increasing closeness to the hills, plains, valleys and seas of Africa.

***

It is because I am filled with such a deep sense of passion for Africa that I feel that I have a responsibility to share it.

I am encouraged to write by the thought that my joy might light a spark in someone else's soul, which in turn could ignite their romance with Africa.

JUNE
1976

SOUNDS

If I were to choose one sound to describe the Africa which makes me smile,
It would be the hadeda's strident heralding of the coming night
As he sweeps across the boundless sky.
The most haunting sound of Africa, however,
Jolts my human frame and triggers a primeval sense of earthly attachment.
The sudden piercing cry of the fish eagle arouses a mysterious and deep-seated longing,
Akin to the sadness and yearning one experiences in the abyss of loneliness.
I don't fully understand it,
But believe it is related to our roots in Africa
Which are tangled in a profusion of nostalgic sentiments.

TRUST

When disillusioned with humanity
Remember
Somewhere out there is the shadow of one of God's creatures
He won't let you down.
How can he?
He accepts you for what you are,
And expects nothing more
Than peaceful acceptance of himself.

1

AFRICA

We are the guardians of this mystical place,
But it's vanishing now without a trace,
The crowded plains,
The silent streams,
Are empty fields and wishful dreams.

We are the keepers of this ancient land,
But we're losing touch under human hand,
The living seas,
The forested slopes,
Are barren lakes and shattered hopes.
We are the parents of Africa's sons,
We've been too busy with spears and guns,
The time has come,
For us to fight,
To regain our treasure,
And get it right.

NOVEMBER
1976

I~T WAS A SULTRY EVENING, FAIRLY TYPICAL~ of Zululand, and the distant rumbling promised another downpour. As I leant over the somewhat flimsy wire fencing which separated the rest camp from the reserve a welcome breeze carried a distant animal smell, and I inhaled until my lungs were at bursting point.

There was a good view from where I was standing and I scanned the dense bush for any sign of life. I thought I saw something move, but as soon as my eyes had focused beneath the acacia tree all was still.

It did not matter. I'd only just arrived in Hluhluwe Game Reserve, and tomorrow I too would be on the other side of the fence.

A small group of hadedas flew overhead, their lusty chorus shattering the velvety stillness as they winged their way towards the valley floor. I couldn't help chuckling to myself as the tide of inane laughter echoed, before it ebbed away, lost amongst a blanket of forest.

Hluhluwe takes its name from a plant or thorny climber, and it was here in the small game park nestled amongst rolling hills and valleys that I finally realised the reason for the magnetic pull which had lured me to this ageless land.

The last of the sun's rays were fading as the fiery disc became engulfed by an ominously dark cloud, brooding over the horizon – and then I felt the first drops of rain. There's something different about the rain in Africa. It soothes the fever of the day's pitiless heat and satiates the earth in one brief glut. A million pores gape to suck at the torrent before it recedes with the same suddenness of its arrival. I could smell so much more after a good rain. It was almost as if each leaf, each blade of grass was announcing its thanksgiving by the enhancing of its delicate spices.

I ambled towards our hut stopping briefly to photograph a single impala lily, its head slightly bowed by the weight of a lingering droplet of rain. I knew I was noticing so much more and for the first time in my life I was beginning to think, to really contemplate the complexities of creation, and how, in a world so orientated to materialism, the jewels of nature's realm, which had always been but gone unnoticed, were taking on a new meaning in my life.

The dividing line between night and day in Africa is a thin one; dusk is transient and just as one relaxes to enjoy it, it's gone. The intrusion of a world of darkness has taken over, bringing with it a whole new euphony of mysterious sounds and vital expressions from a world of the unseen. Fireflies busily went about their business, tiny luminous beacons of light betraying their presence as they danced across the night sky. Without the fluorescent spark I would never have known of their existence, and I considered a multitude of life forms unbeknown in their secrecy.

An eerie yapping in the distance broke my train of thought, a sound carried by a favourable wind, probably over a distance of miles. Jackal! At last I was actually hearing it, seeing it, smelling it and feeling it! I was face to face with the heart of Africa! I was in paradise!

That night I couldn't sleep. I was too alert. The atmosphere of Hluhluwe had awakened my very soul, and I didn't want to miss anything. The heat of the day lingered long into the night, and I kicked off the sheets, exposing more flesh for the bloodthirsty mosquitoes which had somehow penetrated the protective screen at all the windows and doors. From my bed I watched the pale moonrise which emphasised the mystical effect of bush life. It cast pastel shades of light across a navy blue sky, and I must have watched a hundred clouds of cotton wool pass over it before a night owl appeared in perfect silhouette as it hurried on its way in search of a meal.

I had no idea that my love affair with Africa was just beginning.

DECEMBER
1976

A Painted Lady is gently born
Upon a fluted breeze.
She curtseys down upon her knees
And prays upon Christ's thorn...

Small as I am
Please don't let anything crush me.

JANUARY
1977

THERE WAS NO WARNING. I SHOULDN'T HAVE been out of the car because I knew the regulations of the park forbade it, but I'd spotted a huge crocodile sunning itself on a sandbank mid-river, and I wanted a photograph. Having secured my vantage point and positioned myself to 'shoot' at this much maligned and supposed villain of the African river, my friend yelled, "Move!" I felt the blood leach from the very vault of my being and a wave of fear launched itself, rocketing through every muscle that my body owned. Lowering my camera I could see that the crocodile hadn't moved, so what was it?

I turned and saw it. A prehistoric effigy, a sold mass of leathery hide had broken cover and was crossing the road towards me. I hadn't reckoned on this kind of electric thrill so soon! There was no time to collect my camera gear, and whilst my friend blew the horn in an attempt to distract the rhino I bolted for the safety of the car. As I slammed the car door firmly shut, I was able to take stock of its enormous dimensions as it casually approached and began scraping its conoid protrusion against the bumper of the vehicle.

This was Umfolozi: a sheltered haven for the white rhino which was plucked from the brink of extinction by the world-famous Operation Rhino in the 1960s. Normally not aggressive like its black cousin the white rhino relieved its curiosity, and after circling the car heaved its hulk far enough away for me to recover my camera equipment, which thankfully lay unharmed at the spot where I had deserted it.

Following the mantle of vegetation which laced the river, we glimpsed a beautiful waterbuck about to succour its thirst at the quiet watering place, his senses alert to any kind of danger which might strike at any time or from any angle. Stopping the vehicle at regular intervals, switching off the motor and winding down the windows endowed us with more rewards than trying to cover the greatest possible distance in an attempt to see 'everything'.

My most vivid recollections stem from the times when we just sat, deep within the reserve, where we were able to appreciate our close bond with the flesh and blood of nature's real world. The slightest sound of a snapping twig or the muted rustle of the grass disturbed by something on the move would penetrate the intense silence and bring us back to a state of readiness whereupon we hardly dare breathe. This is when I could feel the warm excitement mounting in my blood, not knowing if we were in the path of a determined buffalo, if a snake was slithering its way through the undergrowth, or if the reclusive bushbuck was about to disclose itself. We had to wait but our vigilance was usually rewarded, simply I think, because our stationary vehicle was not perceived as a threat. The game seemed blithely unaware of our being there. Conversely, and sometimes unknowingly, we found ourselves the subject of much scrutiny; we don't know for how long two mongooses had been peering at us from behind a small mound, but as soon as they realised that they had been spotted they scampered for cover and vanished, absorbed by the dense network of shrubs.

One of the most imposingly beautiful sights I have ever had the joy to behold was looking out from Mpila hutted camp, pitched on the crest of Umfolozi's territorial sweep. The moulded landscape rolled away to form a switchback of variegated terrain before converging with the placid waters of the Black and White Umfolozi rivers that meandered their sculptured course through bush green and valley deep. The restrictions of the outside world with all its strife seemed so far away, whilst here amidst a small patch of proclaimed wilderness, contentment and freedom filled the air.

From our perch we shared the lofty majesty of so many birds of prey which soared above the eternal abyss, displaying a carefree but tenuous dominance over the sky. With the daily descent of the solar disc through the lilac heavens, dramatic lighting effects enriched the virgin tapestry below us, and the mournful lament of the emerald-spotted wood dove was fluted in despair. "My mother is dead, my father is dead, all my relations are dead, oh, oh, oh, oh."

In the quiet of sunset I acquired what I can only assume to be the birth of my own wisdom and I began an intimacy with all that agonised with the need to survive in a world of human encroachment and 'progression'.

'Courage, Strength and Patience'. This is the English translation of the word 'Umfolozi'. The Zulus demanded these qualities in the man chosen to lead a herd of oxen. I think these are qualities needed in all men so that we might ensure the continuation of all life, no matter what form it takes.

As I picked out the Southern Cross, carved low in the night sky, the familiar wild sounds penetrated the blackness once more, and I prayed that the African night would never be silent.

MARCH
1977

BIRDS OF A FEATHER (I)

In the gaze of the beholder,
There is a place named *Paradise*.
As the ear lends tones
To the sound of *Paradise,*
The soul searches
To blend in *Paradise*
And when we speak it,
With which words do we paint it?

Paradise can fly by us,
In a flash.
Sky shades of orange and blue,
Delicate.
Floating through space,
A trail of velvet plumage loping,
Priceless, mystical, hoping,
As if incognito.
So, what is this *Paradise*
Where does the secret lie?
Ask the flycatcher.
Who has surely transcended,
From Heaven,
A shining gift,
We are all free to follow.

MARCH
1978

I T WAS THE ABSOLUTE QUIETNESS THAT I remember most. There was not a breath of air; the riverbanks and hollows were still shrouded by an early morning mist; it would be some little time before the sun was high enough to percolate the foggy screen.

We nearly missed it!

The perfect camouflage of a nyala bull had almost outwitted us, and yet there he was, dignified and stately in a world where he so rightly belonged. Impeded by my inexperience, I prepared to shoot my film, but before I had a chance to raise the camera to eye level he had retreated to the safety of the densely knotted vegetation. I was disappointed, and I still had no inkling of the patience that I would have to acquire or the perseverance I would need to achieve my goals.

High overhead two bataleur eagles greeted the dawn, soaring on outstretched wings, displaying a certain authority of the infinite sky. As they swooped into a steep dive with determined self-expression, rolling and tumbling with a purposeful precision, I could almost feel their joy.

For every animal that was here in the Kruger National Park there must have been a hundred that went unnoticed, and I found the challenge of discovery irresistible.

The miles of slow motoring in the sub-tropical swelter were worth any discomfort that we endured. Zebra quenching their thirst at a secluded waterhole; the clashing of impala horns in a confrontation of male dominance over a harem of ewes; the chattering of baboons as they romped in playful mood beneath the trees and the restless trotting of a black jackal, barely visible amidst the canopy of shrubs.

The harsh world of survival was all around me, and I began to see the hunter and the hunted as an integral necessity for the preservation of the continuing species. Life and death would come to each and every animal, bird and insect, but in nature's own time, without harmful interference from man, and it seemed so right.

It was whilst parked on a rise overlooking Kumana Dam, south of Satara Camp, that we watched spellbound as 'Life in an African Game Reserve' played itself out. As we surveyed the placid scene in front of us where a herd of waterbuck enjoyed the warmth of the ripening sun, we suddenly became aware of two beautiful felines that were using our vehicle for cover as they too watched over the waterhole – their intention obvious. My friend whispered, "Cheetah," and I froze in my seat, hardly daring to breathe. I was aware of my thumping chest caused by a sudden gush of adrenaline released within me. My inner voice screamed out with an indescribable joy – I wanted all my family and friends in other parts of the world to enjoy this with me, so they too could experience this truly African moment.

Safely locked inside our human lair I looked on wide-eyed and speechless as the two experts manoeuvred themselves. Crouching low, one cheetah slunk away to the left of us, whilst the other veered to the right. Once they had reached the savannah they were hardly visible to us; their slow but steady progress, bodies lithe and hugging the ground, could only be discerned by the gentle movement of the tall grass. With the cheetah now fifty metres apart and circling the innocent scene there must have been some telepathic communication as they revealed themselves simultaneously to make a high-speed dash towards their target.

It was as if I had been transported to another dimension, because nothing in my life, so far, had come close to the intensity of the feelings that I was experiencing now. In a fraction of a second the reaction of those in the pathway of the thrusting attack seemed desperate. Pandemonium ensued as waterbuck, impala, warthog and zebra made a bid to escape amidst a pall of thick dust. The cheetah made contact with a female waterbuck, slowed by her pregnant status, tripped her and attempted to gain a stranglehold around her neck.

My emotions were conflicting, and I wasn't sure what I wanted to witness. As the tears began to trickle down my cheeks in sympathy with the waterbuck, the most amazing thing occurred. A male waterbuck, in full flight, stopped, turned and made a dash for the desperate scene. With head down and horns ready to impale the enemy, it charged the cheetah. A brief foray ensued, but within moments the cheetah had retreated, which allowed the shocked but otherwise unharmed waterbuck to rise to her feet, regain her dignity, and trot away to the safety of the herd.

The cheetah looked on in disbelief. Exhausted, but in perfect unison with shoulders touching, they slowly walked to the water's edge. Having quenched their thirst, they sought the dappled shade of a small acacia tree, where they lay down. Only the occasional flick of a black and white tail above the grass betrayed their presence. For anyone else who stopped at Kumana Dam, there was now nothing to suggest that anything had taken place. I felt very smug!

BUSH WATCH

In the clearing of a misty hollow
A herd of springbok graze.
The air is still, the sky cloudless,
There is a waterhole beyond.
This is a well-trodden path –
Silently a lioness pervades the calm,
Stalking – nostrils flared –
The tall grass barely moves.
Her prey already targeted
They know of nothing sinister.
The scene is set,
The audience seated,
The curtain rises,
The climax is close –
"Go away" they scream from lofty boughs,
"Go away" the grey bird cries.
The buck looks up.
The lioness halts.
The loeries saved the day.

AN EVENING DRIVE FROM SHINGWEDZI CAMP TOOK me to a spot which revealed the simplicity and naturalness which belongs to the very heart of Africa.

No words could lend colour to the perfect grace which existed before my very eyes. Beneath a verdant umbrella overlooking the riverbed vervet monkeys quietly relaxed. A handful appeared involved with important discussions as they sat face-to-face displaying human-like gestures of concentration, good humour and at times, disagreement. Mothers were absorbed in nursing their infants, painstakingly combing their coats for ticks and fleas which once discovered not only relieved the baby's itch, but provided a tasty snack for 'mum' who relished the juicy morsel.

Sub-adults, full of self-importance, demonstrated their arboreal versatility; for the most part it was a friendly test of skills, but like children every now and then a scuffle

11

would break out which preceded a noisy quarrel and a precarious treetop chase! Large male monkeys, oblivious of the adolescent skirmishes, lolled prostrate, limbs splayed and eyes closed, indulging themselves in their languor. In a couple of hours, when night would slowly steal the light of day once more, these same monkeys would be alert to the dangers of the heart of darkness, and on guard against their deadliest enemy, the leopard.

A nyala calf, still innocent and vulnerable, unwittingly startled a young monkey intent on plucking the petals from a single flower. It leapt up, tail curled, emitting a terrified scream as it fled. Bedlam followed. The tranquil scene was transformed into a state of confusion and chaos. Monkeys screeched as they ran for the safety of the trees, whilst the bewildered nyala panicked in a frantic search for its mother. Fear spread rapidly, and in an instant the riverbed was devoid of life.

A grey loerie noisily left its perch squawking its "Go away" warning call as it strained for the security of the sky. We, however, stayed on until the watery light rendered photography impossible.

Driving back, as we neared the camp, we stopped the car to savour the setting sun before it was swallowed up by the yawning horizon. The bush was stained with a golden glow which becalmed the threat of darkness and which was the timekeeper for the start of another hunt. A dainty steenbok grazed in solitude, stopping occasionally to cast an eye in our direction. I hoped that he would not be the hunted one tonight and that he would live to see the glory of another day.

The stars hung so low that night that I felt that I could almost touch them. As we sat around the campfire and listened to the ticking of the bush I knew that at last I had broken free. From now on, whenever I could no longer tolerate the polluted and stifling effects of city life, I would find contentment and spiritual release amongst the living wild, wherever that might be.

MAY
1980

BIRDS OF A FEATHER (11)
It's a uniquely obscure sound
Uttered from a concealed stage.
Acoustically enveloping
A master of ventriloquism.
It rises and falls,
It announces a change
In the weather.
It's the rainbird.
The Coucal.
Oh! Ancient bird of Africa
Thank you for your prophesy.
Your omen is enough.
You are the harbinger of life blood,
For the veins of African soil.

BIRDS OF A FEATHER (III)

Drifting.

Winding.

Ascending from the valley

Is a cry –

It ebbs and flows.

Is born and grows.

What is the sound I've heard?

Sailing.

Pitching.

Descending from the summit

Is a cry –

A lonely pining.

Monotonous whining.

What is this sound that's erred?

Weaving.

Swerving.

Straining through the gulleys

Is a cry –

A baby wailing?

A trumpet hailing?

No! It's the hornbill bird.

JUNE
1980

A CRISP WINTER'S MORNING AND WE WERE ON the trail to Mkuze, a small game reserve tucked away in the northern reaches of Zululand, east of the Lebombo Mountains. Once off the main road the dusty track was in an appalling condition, parts of it having disintegrated, leaving gaping craters and deep trenches which weren't always easy to negotiate. It humped its way over rocky scarps at rakish angles and wedged its way through dense, low-lying bush which clawed at our vehicle as it passed by. It cut through neat African kraals still bathed in the dewy haze of early morning, where we waved to inquisitive children and narrowly missed colliding with wandering livestock. The further we went the more primitive it became, and I felt Mkuze was going to be the ideal location from where I could continue to study and photograph the wildlife.

We pitched our tent and made camp about eight kilometres from the main hutted camp, where it was peaceful, basic and secluded; in fact, just the way we wanted it, because from now on we wished to be as close to the core of nature as possible, which meant we would be sleeping out beneath the stars.

As soon as the explosive heat of midday had abated we started out in the direction of Malibali Hide, leaving a spiralling twister of fine red dust in our wake, which clung to the heavy air. Only minutes had elapsed when we spotted a two-metre cobra slithering across the sandy road only metres in front of us. Almost on top of it we braked, and simultaneously the cobra reared up, spreading its hood in a threatening display of aggression. I had never seen a venomous snake in its natural habitat and was amazed at the height of its vertical challenge. Satisfied that we posed no danger it retreated, slid into the grass, and was gone without a trace. Already I was having reservations about camping out!

Mkuze proved to be an ornithologist's dream, and at Malibali a party of red-faced mousebirds clambered amongst the branches of a small tree, noisily exchanging their shrill vocal passions, whilst a saddle-billed stork waded ankle deep around the edge of the waterhole, occasionally stabbing at the surface with its long bill in pursuit of a passing small fish or frog, perhaps.

At Bube Hide the waterhole was never devoid of life, and whilst a myriad of birds, reptiles and small mammals made their home here there was a continual coming and going of visitors. A big crocodile lay placidly at the water's edge, its mouth slightly ajar, which enabled a common sandpiper to peck at the jagged weaponry within, which not only cleaned the croc's teeth, but provided the plucky bird with a never-ending supply of food. A grey heron strutted around the water's edge, and then after a short burst of flight it landed amongst the lilies in the middle of the waterhole, where it remained motionless, with its long neck extended, ready for the swift action so necessary to secure its prey.

Neither was the place ever totally silent. Very close to the hide a family of Egyptian geese hissed and quacked; with three young chicks to look after, only one adult at a time would wander off to feed so that the youngsters were never left unguarded. When they took to the water one parent led the fleet, whilst the other protectively brought up the rear; it was a perfect family setting.

Msinga Hide was equally blessed with its share of water birds. A green-backed heron arrived mid-afternoon and perched on a tree stump that was protruding above the surface of the water. It remained stock-still for over an hour before it snatched a tiny frog from beneath the surface with lightning speed.

Wildebeest and zebra came in single file to take a long drink prior to nightfall. The ungainliness of the wildebeest seemed to enhance the natural beauty of the zebra, the latter of which I always found to be so photogenic.

Long after the zebra had left the waterhole we could hear their intermittent honking in the distance as they prepared to face the dangers of another night in the bush. A great white heron glided in and made a streamlined landing as it skimmed across the water. Every now and then its long neck plunged below the surface to retrieve a ready food supply unobtainable by most birds of prey. Nyala at all stages of maturation wandered down to drink at regular intervals, sometimes sinking up to their knees in the boggy mire at the edge of the pan.

Just as we were about to leave a solitary grey duiker appeared. Shy and nervous, he attempted to drink several times but he never quite made it, only to disappear into obscurity again.

Travelling back to camp that evening we were alerted by a crowded sky of vultures circling at different levels. We stopped to survey the flat open grassland stretching out into oblivion. With binoculars we were able to pick out several jackals, but could see no sign of an actual kill. Several kilometres further on two cheetah were cutting through the tall grass. As we stopped they mounted a small kopje and we could see that their bellies were bloated. We deduced that these magnificent cats had been responsible for the kill back on the plain.

The nights spent in Mkuze were exciting; being outside, all the sounds and smells were heightened, and when noises became a little too close we would shine the torch into the blackness, only to see many pairs of eyes looking in our direction. One night I had to visit the ablutions, which were about fifty metres from where we were camped. Something warm and furry brushed past my leg, and although it was probably a jackal, I shall never know for sure.

JULY

1980

TWENTY-FOUR HOURS

As the first light dawns
In the Eastern skies,
A grey dove mourns,
Spreads its wings and flies.

As the dark sky fades
Dressed in glowing hues,
A thrush parades,
Whilst it spreads good news.

As the sun appears
Changing night to day,
The ibis cheers
As he drifts away.

As the last star pales
In the morning light,
The cuckoo hails
On his maiden flight.
As the brightness grows
Deep into the morn,
A raven crows,
His job is to warn.

The heat, after noon
Pervades the cool.
The sunbirds strewn
Round the nectar pool.

As the Berg winds blow
Through the valley floor,
The eagles know
They've been here before.

As the drops of rain
Begin their descent,
The coucal strains
Unknown as he went.

As the storm explodes
With a fearsome might,
The loerie goads
"Take shelter tonight."

As the day disappears
The twilight becalms,
A robin nears
Singing hymns and psalms

As dusk cloaks the scene,
Hiding all from sight.
The owl has been
Alone on his flight.

In the silence of night,
Divinely discreet.
A whispering plight comes,
As the nightjars meet...

APRIL

1981

AN AFRICAN DAWN

There is an innocence which comes with the dawn.

A quiet gentleness which stirs that little known ardour

Deep within us,

And with its slow and poetic arousal

Comes a sense of relentless passion

Which sustains us throughout the harshness of the day.

MAY

1981

I T WAS THE DRY SEASON IN ONE of the last remaining game reserves where animals rule and man is the guest. To add to the desiccation there was a drought and all life forms were struggling for survival. It had taken us four days to cover the three thousand kilometres from Durban to the wilderness in the northern extremity of Namibia.

For several years it had been my own private dream to visit Etosha (the literal meaning being Great White Place), the main focal point being a dried-up lake known as Etosha Pan. Over the centuries this pan had become dehydrated as rivers from the north, which once quenched its thirst, desisted.

Our vehicle was well equipped for the desert conditions of Namibia and for carrying large quantities of food and water, but most importantly it had been modified by means of a sunroof and ample window space for my growing preoccupation with photography. The only discomfort was the relentless heat and the constant onslaught of a fine powdery dust which violated every conceivable opening into the vehicle as we travelled the mainly untarred roads. It was, of course, an area engaged in a guerrilla war, but there was little to show of this, and I certainly didn't feel threatened by it.

Entering Etosha from its southern boundary, our first camp was made at Okaukuejo which had been established by the side of a floodlit spring from where numerous species of game could be seen drinking both by day and at night. Here too was a water tower which afforded a panoramic view over the sunbaked mopane trees and parched bushveld for as far as the eye could see. From the top (accessible by steps) it was easy to conceive the Great White Place. In the far distance a car, seen only as a small dot, moved, leaving a trail of dust in its wake which lingered in the languid air. Just visible to the naked eye was a herd of giraffe moving onto the plains, their tall necks revealed by the backdrop of the blue sky. The stillness could be seen in shades of white.

The silence was soon broken by a noisy display flight of two black korrhans passing overhead, common birds with a love of the dry open savannah. Although from this ideal viewing position we could see so little in the way of animal life, we knew that the untamed country that we were looking out over supported a myriad of creatures, and I contemplated the words of Ralph Waldo Emerson: 'Nothing is great but the inexhaustible wealth of nature.'

Etosha is also meant to mean 'Place of Mirages' and as we gazed towards the salt-encrusted clay base of the pan its edge seemed to take on a liquid form which merged with the sky to produce a shimmering horizon. From here the pan looked to be full of water, and I now knew what it was to witness a mirage.

Exhausted by our long journey, we decided to stay in camp for the rest of the day so that we could prepare ourselves for an early start the next morning. For me there is nothing more exhilarating than being part of the African bush at night. The tropical darkness heralds a symphony of its own, unsurpassed by the world's greatest musicians. My senses tingle and become alert to all that surrounds me. Life goes on around the clock, and it is at night that some species become more active, whilst others emerge from their hideaways where they have spent the daylight hours asleep. Night beetles and cicadas strike up their continuous song at dusk, and proceed with the cacophony for many hours.

As the night progresses, one can, through sound, catch a glimpse of what is happening 'out there'. The howling of excited jackal or the whooping of a pack of hyena is commonly used as a method of locating each other, especially when there has been a kill. Lions are at their most active at night, a time when they frequently make their kills. There is nothing to match the shattering of the African night's silence more than the full-bellied roar of a mature lion.

We had not long settled by the campfire, our appetites assuaged by grilled meat and our thirsts quenched by chilled white wine, when a low rumbling sound drifted over towards us from the direction of the spring. Excited by this strange noise we ran to a place of safety beside this secluded watering place with camera, lenses and tripod.

A formidable sight greeted us. Four massive bull elephants stood knee deep in the water, sucking up vast volumes of fluid through their trunks and pouring it down their throats. In the assimilated moonlight, effected by the dimmed floodlights, we were able to observe these monumental creatures naturally and without their awareness of our presence. We sat in the warm air watching their antics until they lumbered off into the night, their enormous hulks carried silently on large cushioned feet.

In the wings were a family of giraffe, and after awaiting the departure of the elephants they now nervously approached the waterhole. We were witnessing the 'rights to drink' ritual, and we saw very few animals who were brave enough to drink alongside elephants. Unlike the fearlessness of their predecessors, the giraffe were alert to the slightest sound; a cough or spoken word would send them loping back into the cover of the bush. Giraffe are at their most vulnerable when stooping to drink and therefore have to be convinced that it is safe to do so.

22

After some considerable time and various attempts at lowering their bodies into position they finally drank in quick succession. The contrast of the two species was so evident; the leisurely romp of the elephants compared with the hesitant brevity of the giraffes' liquid revival. As they moved off the water's surface became quiescent, the tension eased and only the lingering redolence of the elephant remained in the still of the night.

WHISPERS OF THE SOUL

Listen to the whispers
Of the voice within your soul.
There is no better magic
To bind you as a whole.

Surrender to the thoughts
Which echo in your heart
For they will yield a footpath
When lost or far apart.

Behold the love within,
So nurture what you feel.
It is a gift that's sacred
And it has a gold seal.

DREAMS AND SUNSETS

Have you ever loved someone or somewhere so much
That you wanted to tell the world?
Have you ever cried as you watched the sun setting
Casting a kaleidoscope of orange and pink rays
Over your misty world?
In the flickering moments of the sleepy sun's light
Have you ever travelled a million miles
And dreamed of living forever?
As the flaming tones fade,
Have they ever reflected the nostalgia within you,
Yet rekindled the belief that nothing is out of reach
And that dreams are the gateway to your goals?
As the Earth's womb falls beneath the horizon,
Leaving you surrounded by darkness,
Have you ever asked God to help you share your
Warmth and light indiscriminately
And to show you how to keep the love
That life has brought you?
Dreams and sunsets live side-by-side.
They come and go.
They are beautiful.
They are Life.

"AFRICA, I CAN'T LEAVE YOU," WERE THE first words that entered my mind as my first day in Etosha dawned. A balloon of ruby red had broken from its mooring and was now sailing silently above the horizon. This peaceful passage was steering through an expanse of cloudless sky above plains and thorn trees and very quickly it began to glide gently into the shimmering morning air.

The golden helm's journey transformed night into day as it ascended through transient shades of crimson, amber and yellow, leaving a glowing sea of calm in its wake. I marvelled at the richness of this wild reach, where the rewards manifested themselves in the form of the intangible. To take refuge here was a course in self-discovery and expression. It allowed one the opportunity to achieve an infinite patience and determination, and equipped one with the ability to experience the very essence of the affinity which unites all living things.

My love of photography endowed me with an enthusiastic anticipation, compelling me to rise in the darkness of pre-dawn, so that I could be on the road as the first rays of light illuminated the harsh and diverse wilderness. It was as if I were witnessing the dawn of creation every day.

Two miles out of camp, and north of the Ondundozonananandana Hills, we were alerted by a lone giraffe's agitated behaviour. With the aid of binoculars we were able to discern the reason. Crouching low on the grass on a slight elevation was a large golden-maned lion. We scanned the grassy plains for any accomplices to what we thought might be a kill. We were positive that the remainder of the pride must be close, as no lion alone could bring down and maintain a death hold on a giraffe. But after some considerable time the cat-and-mouse tactics continued, and we began to realise that there were no other lions, and the manner in which the lion was now exposing himself confirmed there would be no such kill!

We proceeded to Leeubron waterhole, preparing ourselves to await any arrivals. Already there were two blacksmith plovers strutting around the water's edge, foraging for anything edible. Warthog, unashamed in their ugliness, tottered in single file, tails erect, on their way to drink. A jackal, ears pricked and keen eyes staring, encircled the vehicle, first one way and then the other. Whilst his attention was firmly fixed on us, a diminutive steenbok which we had not spotted in the camouflage of the shrub took the chance to spring to safety, stopping briefly at a more secure distance to turn around and take a long hard look, its beautifully marked ears outstretched in an almost horizontal attitude, before disappearing.

With the steenbok safely gone we watched amused as the jackal made futile and frustrated attempts to attack several cackling guinea fowl which, on each occasion that they felt threatened, ran haphazardly and then forced a brief burst of flight into the lower branches of the trees.

Engrossed in this spectacle I was totally unaware of what had arrived and had been sitting and staring at my exposed back through the open window of the vehicle. I must have sensed something, for when I turned around I felt an icy chill shudder through my whole being as I met eyeball-to-eyeball with the lion we previously had been watching back on the plains. Through the small space of air that separated us I could smell his fetid breath. He was an arm's length away from me!

Each day brought its own rewards, and although capturing the wildlife on film was a major requisite for me there were times when photography was neither possible nor pertinent, and in those instances it was always a refreshing change just to sit back and relax and let the world of Etosha live on all around us, unrecorded. Almost without exception, however, the permanent reminders of the wildlife that I did capture on film could never have been taken without the loyalty, skill and encouragement of my friend and driver, who always seemed able to react swiftly to all my commands of "Stop!", "Go!", "Back a bit!", "Switch off!" Not only this, however, she also encouraged, supported and anticipated my needs and feelings as a photographer. The joys of sharing were heightened in a world where one was surrounded by nature's beauty and freedom.

AWARENESS

Life without love is walking in the rain
And not getting wet.
It is an ocean without waves.
A desert with no sand.

Love without recognition is drawing the blinds
On a sunny day.
It is a flower without perfume.
A bird with no song.

Recognition without understanding is seeing a rainbow
And not counting the colours.
It is a clock without hands.
A story with no end.

When life hands you love
Recognise it with your eyes.
Understand it with your heart.
And trust in it forever.

A GIFT OF GRACE

To be able to find some meaning

Is a jewel

Of innocence

And awareness.

To experience a sense of love

Is the gift

Which is given

To embrace us.

To treasure some time in wonderment

Is a joy

And a blessing

Bestowed on us.

To release a flow of gentle tears

Is a share

And a measure

Of completeness.

To know the reward of acceptance

Is a Grace

Of our spirit

To redeem us.

TODAY WE LEFT FOR HALALI CAMP.

At about 9 a.m. we arrived at the Ondongab waterhole. As we approached a regal kudu bull and his calf looked up, water dripping from their lips. It was one of the most beautiful sights that I had ever seen. These majestic buck blended with the foliage, the effect enhanced by the stark whiteness of the pan behind them. In the distance a herd was approaching, identification made difficult by the mirroring effect of the salty flatness.

As they neared it became obvious that this was a herd of zebra, in numbers such as I had never seen before. I could not believe that herds of this size still existed. There must have been a thousand. But then this was Etosha, and one of the few places on earth where enormous migrations took place, a phenomenon controlled by an inborn instinct to survive.

Within half an hour of our arrival at Ondongab the waterhole was a merging picture of black and white, and a revelation of life, and for us, a uniquely special experience.

It was only after we had spent about an hour at Ondongab that we noticed a python in a small leafless tree about six metres in front of us. We were amazed at how this reptile had concealed itself from us camouflaged by its perfect disguise as a branch. Entwined around the slender trunk, its head was poised motionless at the tip of the uppermost branch, an ideal place from which to launch its attack and make a strike at an unsuspecting passing bird.

Horrified, we watched a host of small birds flying to and fro, within inches of the python's head. Then, like lightning, the snake struck, and with one swift stab into the airspace his meal was procured. Rendered still and silent, any pathetic gestures of life which shuddered from within the weaver's body were crushed by the python's grip, and then the moment of death, as the weaver's head fell backwards, limp and spiritless. The little victim was then lubricated with a viscous fluid and swallowed without delay or effort.

Only forty seconds had elapsed between the bird's ill-fated flight and its complete and utter disappearance. It was heart-rending to see a second weaver hovering over the death scene, cheeping incessantly in defiance of the cruel taking of his mate. With only the bulging of his body to show for what had taken place, the python stealthily descended the tree, and slunk away to digest his meal in private.

JUNE

1981

JOURNEY OF LIFE

Looking beyond what appears to be.
To travel life's natural spoor.
To reach above the darkening clouds,
From a mountain or a moor.

Releasing all that is trapped inside.
To be striving at all cost,
To give the Earth a warm embrace
So the spirit can't be lost.

THE BULBUL

No-one heard, you weren't seen,
Silent dive – Gymnogene –
Innocent prey, a mother's watch
Lapsed for a moment, such a loss.
Torn from bough, tiny chick,
Clawed from nest, t'was so quick –
Shadow that your wings created
Caused untold fear, choirs abated.
Stolen child, sickening sight,
Wedged between talons, tight,
Hanging limply, a sense of doom.
A cruel life, since its mother's womb.
Race is on, mother's left
Her nursery perch, bereft.
She cries and screams, bombarding you
"My only child, this can't be true".
There's no match, Gymnogene,
The Bulbul, so to glean,
Her infant now a tasty meal
Life's cycle harsh, woeful, but real.

AFTER A WEEK OF BEING IN ETOSHA we had seen most species from the tiny ground squirrel to the mighty elephant, but we were still searching for both leopard and cheetah. Then one morning between Noniams and Goas we spotted a magnificent cheetah, outstretched and relaxing right by the side of the road. The motor engine was switched off and we coasted to a point which we felt would not disturb the snoozing feline. Inevitably she stirred, and she was beautiful. As we gazed at each other I could clearly see the pupils of her eyes.

In between the sightings of the larger mammals I became endeared to the smaller feathered creatures, and can relate my present love of ornithology directly to Etosha. One of the more boldly coloured birds, the crimson-breasted shrike, added a brilliant splash of colour to the otherwise dull appearance of the dry bush. Violet-eared and black-cheeked waxbills also demonstrated a rare loveliness, whilst the Meyer's parrots clad in green and yellow congregated in pairs amongst the fruiting trees, where they vocalised their harsh screams prior to winging their flight.

For me, there is nothing more intimidating than rounding a bend and being confronted by a six-tonne wall of elephant hide which is blocking the entire road! With narrow roads and waterholes so close to these roads, this was not an unfamiliar encounter.

At Kalkheuwel a mock charge by an enormous matriarch happened with deceptive suddenness. With her trunk held high in an attempt to catch wind of our scent, and with her ears outstretched to intensify her foreboding threat, she made her challenge with a churning up of the dust underfoot and then, alarmingly, a dramatically imposing mock charge.

Although we knew of very few instances where an elephant had pursued the intimidation, for me it remained a daunting experience, and a very real cause to maintain nerves of steel.

It was here at Kalkheuwel that we observed the well-documented greeting ceremony between a lone bull that had been revelling in his midday aquatic pleasures and this same formidable old matriarch who had been leading her herd to drink as we arrived. There were thirteen elephants at various stages of maturation, the youngest of which was still small enough to walk between its mother's legs. This was a touching sight, and despite the young calf's tiny stature it mimicked its elders in every way, although sucking up water through its immature trunk proved tiring, so it had to resort to sucking from its mother's teats.

The lone bull made a premature retreat from the waterhole and headed into the surrounding vegetation, a manoeuvre closely observed by the matriarch. After a few minutes the bull re-emerged and was immediately approached by the female elephant, her trunk held high. As they closed in on each other their fast determined strides portrayed an imminent clash, and yet instead a silent and wonderfully expressive form of communication took place. They linked trunks as if shaking hands and any amount of intimate gestures ensued. Consequently, the bull acknowledged his acceptance by rejoining the herd and continuing to enjoy his ablutions.

For me, this is where it all started. I felt akin to nature and its life force. It was no wonder to me that some of the most passionate feelings originate in Africa.

A LAND AT WAR

For another day
I know I am here.
I am looking at Africa,
What is it I fear?
The sky stays so blue.
I smell the perfume.
I'm believing my senses,
Why is there such gloom?
Sunrise so early,
It warms to my heart.
The Orb Spider was spinning
When the night made its start.
The dew seems to shine
No matter my care,
Thinking back to creation
A world rich and rare.
Birdsong so happy.
Uplifting and bright.
Original symphony
So why do we fight?
Love all around me
An honour bestows
I don't want this land to be
Changed, my God knows.
To reconcile thoughts
Reality dares
To continue the challenge
For sharing my cares.

Late one afternoon we drove to Klein Okevi, a waterhole close to the Namutoni rest camp. We arrived just at the wrong time, as unwittingly we found ourselves in the direct line of a lioness's charge. Prior to our untimely appearance she must have patiently waited in the surrounding bush for a herd of zebra to come and drink, and then, just as she had chosen her victim and stalked it to within striking distance, we drove up.

The zebra scattered amidst a cloud of dust, their panic-stricken honking audible for some considerable time afterwards. The lioness stood motionless, bemused and startled by our presence, before retiring into the thick cover, tired and panting.

Shortly afterwards two rangers arrived, and they told us that the lioness had a cub, and that she was known to make a kill about once in every three days, and usually at this waterhole. They added that it would be worthwhile to 'stick it out', as having attempted a kill it was obvious that she was hungry and would try again. Nothing happened for the remainder of the evening. We decided to return the next day.

At 6.30 a.m. we watched the sunrise over Klein Okevi tinting the water in pinking hues, and by 7.30 a.m. we had been joined by two hyenas which drank and skulked around the immediate vicinity, sniffing at the ground as they went. We wondered perhaps if our lioness had killed in the night. However the hyenas disappeared and we continued to wait, watching over a completely silent and lifeless waterhole.

Then suddenly, after four and a half hours of apprehensive expectancy, she appeared, proud and dignified in her sovereignty over Klein Okevi. A few moments later she emitted a low moan, and from behind a bush tumbled a young cub, no more than three or four months old. Our patience had been rewarded, and the joy of seeing the two together lolling in the sun surpassed anything I had experienced in the untamed world of the wild.

Energy was quickly sapped in the intense heat, and after a brief drink they wandered over to a large bush, concealing themselves from anything that might also come to quench its thirst.

In optimistic spirit we anticipated a repeat performance of what we had curtailed the day before. After about half an hour had elapsed a family of kudu cautiously approached; it was obvious from their watchful advances and the intermittent snorting of the male that all was not well in their minds. Was it possible that the slight breeze blowing was betraying the lioness's presence?

Eventually they became more settled, which enabled the lioness to make her move. With belly hugging the ground, and her sleek body surrounded by a canopy of vegetation, she inched her way to a more advantageous position behind a large fallen tree trunk. Once convinced that her manoeuvre had gone unnoticed by the kudu she somehow communicated with her cub, evoking its carefully negotiated rendezvous with herself.

It was now obvious that we were watching a lesson in 'pre-kill tactics'. As if to show praise and encouragement of the cub, the lioness licked and fondled it until she returned to the vigil of the kudu's attendance. But the excitement was all too much for the cub, and in a state of youthful oblivion it stood up and ran out into the open, stampeding the kudu instantly.

We were exasperated, and yet we observed that no remonstrations with the little cub ensued; the lioness seemed to blithely take it all in her stride. We sat it out until 6 p.m. that evening, during which time a similar event took place, but there was to be no kill for us. We were quite despondent! When we returned the next morning scraps of hide and a leg bone confirmed that our lions had killed in the night.

THE UNLEASHED PASSION OF YOUTH

The unleashed passion of youth
Does not wane with ageing
It simply becomes more selective
Or emerges as an art form.

OUR TWO WEEKS IN ETOSHA WERE FILLED with mostly heart-warming experiences, but sadly, one scene that we came across sickened our souls and reiterated in our minds the cruel and destructive ways that man has perpetrated.

We had never seen a dead elephant before, and the sight that beset us will remain with me for as long as I live. A solitary lion guarded the carcass, bereft of tail, trunk and feet and mutilated almost beyond recognition. Attempting to discern the sequence of events that had taken place we enquired at the ranger's camp office.

Apparently the elephant had been found wandering with its right foreleg almost severed by a snare, which in turn, had been attached to a sizable tree trunk. From its tracks it was estimated that the elephant had been snared in a notorious poaching area north of the pan, and the pitiful giant had trekked about seventy kilometres across the width of the pan to the safety of the reserve.

Its suffering must have been intolerable. Naturally the rangers had no choice but to put it out of its misery, stripping it of its souvenir potential (tails are made into fly whisks, trunks into wallets and feet into table legs) which would provide extra revenue for the maintenance of Etosha's wildlife sanctuary.

Unfortunately and quite unjustifiably the wildlife of not only Africa but of the whole world is at the mercy of humanity, probably the most selfish and interfering species ever created.

If only *we* lived by some of the rules governed by the animal kingdom the world would be a better place for all of us. It seems to me that we have a lot to learn from those that we are exterminating... but soon it will be too late. The future of man is frightening, for when he has relentlessly rid the earth of everything 'beneath' him, what then?

With that thought in mind, we dreamed of searching for the vast and open spaces of the Okavango Delta.

SEPTEMBER

1981

BIRDS OF A FEATHER (IV)

A sunbird lost her home last night
The little house did fall,
The strands which held the nest to bough
Just had no chance at all.
A sunbird lost her home last night
It stormed the whole night through
It wrenched at twigs and lichen plaques
And dashed them all, but few.
A sunbird lost her home last night
The rains did fall with might,
They soaked the downy feathers
Wrapped snugly out of sight.
A sunbird lost her home last night
Electric charges cost
The lives of three small nestlings
Who from their cot were tossed.
A sunbird lost her home last night
She'll have to start again,
But not till next year, sad to say,
Till then, she'll mourn in pain.

SEPTEMBER
1985

T HE MORE I HAD SEEN OF AFRICA, the more I needed to go on; it had become an intense yearning, the thread of which now ran through my life, binding my innermost conviction and emotions to wild places and the life that those places sustained.

I had been told, "To live the Okavango is to go back to Africa... It has to be lived." Six months later I was on my way to Okavango.

My first impression of Botswana was that of bland flatness accompanied by a feeling of unlimited space and expansiveness. My knowledge of the area was limited, but I contemplated the enigmatical Bushmen, who, since the beginning of life itself, as we know it, had survived the harsh extremes of desert life by using their inherent skills and intimate experience of this wild region.

Three hundred kilometres from Maun, the road head and the springboard from which we would plunge into the Okavango Delta, we approached the stark, untouched and interminable wilderness of the Makgadikgadi Pans. The atmosphere of motionless calm and stillness made me feel alone, and I was aware of my insignificance in this featureless and uninhabited phenomenon which reached out through twelve thousand square kilometres.

Normally a dry salt sheet, the transient flooding of the pan during the occasional 'good year' of rain would provide a rich feeding ground for thousands of flamingos and pelicans, a panache which would flaunt a brilliant splash of colour in an area normally devoid of complexion.

The delicate wind blowing was enough to whip up dust devils, spirals of dry salt reaching for the sky, and as I wandered away from the Land Rover it merged with the elusive effect of the virgin whiteness. In the pregnant silence of the Makgadikgadi I felt my soul was being refreshed. I was aware of the very essence of creation and the spiritual uplift that I was experiencing made me feel privileged to be treading the ground that thousands of wild animals had trodden before me.

Maun emerged as a dusty sprawling town, but it was dusk. We looked longingly at the Thamakalane River which kissed its outskirts. It seemed to greet us knowingly as we drove in from the arid hinterland, and so we proceeded to make camp on its banks, assuaged by the rapidly sinking sun which cast its glowing embers amongst us. Once our appetites had been appeased we retired to the accompaniment of the bell frogs which had already tuned up for the night's orchestral extravaganza. Sleep came easily despite the heat which lingered long into the night.

I was awakened quite naturally by the squabbling of two squirrels as they scampered through the trees above us. Their squeals of delight were heralding the beginning of a new day and I was compelled to rise. Crawling between the tent flaps I could smell the dawn. I wandered down to the river, which was still shrouded by an early morning mist. The eerie screen was no barrier to the 'sound of Africa'. The evoking cry of the fish eagle pierced the screen, revealing an unseen but very definite dominance of its heavenly territory. I could sense its ultimate joy. The sound of silence ensued, and I perceived a deep feeling of belonging. I could feel a warm sense of excitement injecting itself into my bloodstream, achieving the desired effect of an undiluted euphoria. I was intoxicated by a stirring impression of anticipation and hope, and as the sun appeared as a scorched disc above the reeds I was filled with a serene completeness.

Birds of a Feather (V)

As my eyes see your wings of flight
My ears hear your cries of delight
My heart joins with your expression of freedom
And my soul envies your infinite kingdom
Fly.
Don't stop now.
Go.
As only you know how.

OUR FLIGHT FROM MAUN AIRPORT WAS TO take us into the labyrinth of secret waterways and palm-covered islands of the Okavango Swamps. The six-seater, single-engine Cessna taxied to the end of the runway, and in no time at all was straining to render us airborne, with every rivet shuddering and creaking around us. In moments we had passed over the dustbowl of Maun, and a verdant vista of dry land could be seen mingling with sapphire-blue wetlands which stretched out into a boundless infinitude.

From our position in the sky it was easy to view the ever-changing mosaics of narrow streams and wide river courses, breaking and twisting to form a system of channels amongst the flood plains and lagoons, forests and islands, termitaria and papyrus. Dr Livingstone was one of the first explorers to reach this lost world where time stands still, and I felt in a primeval way that I would be seeing this wild and diverse habitat as his eyes had seen it before me, unchanged, unique and in all its pristine glory.

In an area of mystery and ineffable affection where there are no obvious landmarks we landed safely on a short airstrip in the midst of Chief's Island. From here our mode of transport was by dugout canoe (mokoro) which crouched low in the water and was easily overturned if a perfect balance was not maintained.

Each mokoro had been hand-carved from a wild ebony tree by the Botswanan poler, who navigated the multiplicity of waterways by familiarity only. As we glided through thick papyrus and hippo grass we were enveloped by a quiet and stillness so profound that I was aware of every minute sound of the bush. Our mode of conveyance seemed to epitomise the feeling of freedom and I sensed that at last I was actually on equal terms with, and a part of, the living world of the wild.

The absence of artificial sound made it a world to get lost in, a world which glistened in its purity and delicacy, the magic of which had already captivated me.

As kingfishers darted through the reeds and perched on papyrus fronds, a saddle-billed stork stood ankle-deep in water, a lizard struggling to escape its beak. An African jacana strutted amongst the lilies, whilst a green-backed heron foraged at the water's edge prior to a short burst of flight, enabling it to perch on a fallen tree trunk where it remained motionless, its long neck extended, poised and ready for the swift action necessary to secure its prey.

By midday the sun was relentless, so we decided to take advantage of a huge fig tree on the riverbank in order to stretch our legs and to relax further whilst we had lunch. In the distance was a herd of red lechwe browsing in the apparent safety of the savannah-type grassland.

Before too long we were easing our bodies back into the mokoros, whereupon we continued to float amongst the radiance of elegant lilies which supported hundreds of tiny frogs, which in turn lived off mainly flies and mosquitoes. In the crystal-clear sea of water which surrounded us we could see, however, that not all the wonders of the Okavango Delta were above the surface. The meandering and gentle current tugged at a profusion of tangled flora, so beautiful and variegated and equally mystical in the miscellany of life forms that this underwater garden fostered.

Although time was said to stand still in this sheltered haven, I knew that, albeit slowly, the hands of time were moving, and already it seemed too quickly for me. In this paradise of ethereal lustre I was enchanted by the tenuous proof that a world of creatures of the land, water and air were surviving together... and I wanted to stay forever.

BIRDS OF A FEATHER (VI)

Deep in the valley
Hidden from sight
Betrayed by his call
...a flash of white.

Etched against azure
Majesty soars
Preparing to dive
Hunger the cause.

With talons outstretched
The water calm
Beneath the surface
There is alarm.

The peace is jolted
The arrows seize
The fisherman's meal
Procured with ease.

With mighty effort
The raptor rides
Above the glass fields
And killing tides.

Now airborne again
The spirit flies.
Think of this when
The Fish Eagle cries.

S UDDENLY WITHOUT WARNING OUR MOKORO LURCHED, THE placid waters disturbed by a huge circle of ripples, and a frightening turbulence followed.

Then I saw it. A hippo of colossal dimension, and its bulk appeared to pervade the channel for which we were heading. Despite my sheer terror I reached for my camera, and as I did so another head thrust through the surface water. A loud snorting filled the air, followed by a truculent thrashing about, defying us to proceed. Slowly we retreated, which seemed to appease them.

I had heard that many river travellers had lost not only their dugouts but on occasions their lives to these massive jaws and it was justifiably a fate I dare not contemplate. But this was part of the magic of the delta and its blending of opposites... tranquillity and excitement, repose and activity, *dolce far niente* and adventure.

A little further downstream thousands of carmine bee-eaters lined the shore where they tunnelled their nests two metres into the riverbank. They sat in either the branches of the trees, their plumage suffused in shades of pink, red and blue, or on the roots which hung past the entrances to their nests where they serenaded the would-be arrival of their offspring.

Before too long we had reached the designated area where we were to spend the night. Tonight would be the first night that I had spent in a game reserve without even the shelter of a tent. I looked about me with a certain degree of trepidation! The explosive heat of the day was relinquishing its fury and surrounded by the shimmering water we felt the irresistible temptation to respond to its cool embrace. Although hesitant at first, it wasn't long before we had forgotten about the potential hazards and dangers from hippos and crocodiles and were revelling in the translucent waters of the Okavango which caressed our naked bodies... I was in paradise.

The quickly lengthening shadows indicated the advent of the twilight factor, that unequivocal time when every photographer reaches for his camera and every romantic ponders, inspired by the harmony, euphony and glowing beauty.

Again we took to our mokoros. The bush was ticking. The clashing of horns signified a confrontation between two impala rams over a harem of ewes close by. A lone fish eagle flew overhead, calling in its melancholy way, and a troop of baboons warily wandered past in search of safety. In a short while when night would slowly steal the light of day once more, these same baboons would be on their guard, for within the realm of darkness there would come the threat of their deadliest enemy, the leopard.

As we approached a wide lagoon the polers stood perfectly silhouetted by the sinking sun, surely one of the loveliest sights I had ever seen. I was becoming addicted to this natural and uncluttered way of life, and I knew that a part of me would always belong to Africa.

Life Cycle of a Dragonfly

Darting, hither and thither,
You twist with bursts of flight,
Above the watery shallows
Winged beauty at first light.
Hovering over ripples,
You wait at every turn,
Amidst the swamps and reed beds,
A lover to discern.
Sweeping in on wind-songs,
You dive with lightning speed,
Joined in the bond of pleasure,
The passage of your seed.
Returning to your mystic,
In unison you glide,
You know another water nymph
Will in these purls abide.

AFTER SUPPER I BECAME EDGY. I LISTENED to the song of a nightjar which serenaded us from his concealed perch. As people slowly dropped off to sleep, I became mildly irritated. I didn't want to be alone in my wakefulness because I suddenly felt exposed and vulnerable. Lying on my back all I could hear was the sound of my own breathing.

I sat bolt upright! I knew the sound so well – lion – probably a pride of them, but I couldn't judge how close. The low moans, rapid grunts and full-bellied roars seemed close, but in the darkness I could see nothing. *I couldn't believe that everyone slept on!*

I eventually succumbed to sleep, but in no time I was aware of the watery sound of elephant drinking. It was morning. As I ran down to the water's edge I snapped the gossamer threads and silky ribbons of webs, glistening like tinsel between the reeds, a spider's entire night's endeavours torn apart in seconds.

I couldn't see anything but I sensed that the elephant weren't far away. Looking upwards the sky was crowded with vultures, circling at different levels. I presumed that the lion I had heard in the night had killed.

The tempo of bush life was quickening, and this morning we were to explore the island on foot. After about two kilometres we came across trees stripped of their bark, which indicated elephants, and it was these magnificent giants that we were now tracking. We had already inspected large dung heaps, bright yellow and still steaming, signs which indicated their freshness.

It was hot and the humidity thickened the air. We were constantly checking and rechecking the wind as we were now following the unmistakeable spoor of at least four elephants. We spoke in whispers, our senses on full alert. Even the birds were silent. The snapping sound of branches suggested the elephants' proximity, and as we broke cover there, not a hundred metres from us, were four bulls rooting the vegetation in their continual search for food.

Moving in a semi-circle to ensure we were downwind of the elephant we hesitated as two of them stopped eating, a gesture almost immediately followed by the other two, in a manner as if there had been some telepathic communication. We stood stock-still, paralysed by a tacit premonition of uncertainty and impending danger. As four trunks were lifted into the vertical position it was obvious that they had detected our scent, and although my first reaction was to turn tail and run the lead tracker indicated to us to remain as we were.

He put his finger to his lips to portray the importance of remaining mute, at the same time tightening his grip on his spear. After what seemed like an eternity but was in reality only a few minutes, during which time the ears of one of the elephants were extended like huge sails and slapped against its shoulders several times, the foursome moved off, which eased the tension amongst us considerably, although it was some time before we felt at ease to talk to each other again.

After having been on foot for about four hours and having covered quite a distance we decided that it was time to head back for camp. Despite the intense heat and the vast expanse of bush we had been lucky enough to observe over twenty species of game. As we continued in the direction of the camp the leading tracker stopped and pointed. There strolling through the savannah were two cheetah, and as they came into the clearing we could see they had recently eaten. From this we deduced that it was they and not the lions which had been responsible for the kill for which the vultures now lay in wait. We were yet to find the carcass. Several kilometres on we discovered the head and horns of a springbok which had been ravaged by a jackal.

Once back in the camp we stayed put for the rest of the day, and it was an early night for most of us. Mercifully, sleep came easily, and although bush life went on throughout the night I was oblivious to it all, deep in a dreamless slumber. We stayed on Chief's Island for as long as our supplies allowed, but all too soon we were heading back to Maun and 'civilisation', a place I had forgotten existed.

RIVER LIFE

Sit quietly by the river,
Close your eyes
And smell the air.
Remember this is Heaven
And leave it if you dare.
The early mist hangs limply,
From its midst
A Darter glides.
It's heading for the shallows,
A shelter where it hides.
The reeds begin the whisper,
As the breeze
Begins to blow.
The Malachite holds firmly
To the stem he's learnt to know.
A sudden splash hails danger,
From the bank
The other side.
The amber eyes betray it,
Jacanas hitch a ride.
With silent steps, a Bushbuck
Strides gently
From its cover.
Sensing that it's safe to drink
He turns t'wards his lover.
Small circles on the surface,
Tell of fish
That dance below.
Their life so very different
From one their rivals know.
The rumpus from the forest,
The squealing
And the chatter.
The swinging from the treetops
Joyful monkey matter.

44

A piercing yell is stirring,
A sound which seems to echo,
Beyond the bend
There's ructions
Certain to be hippo.
The sounds of life abundant
Impala...
Nothing barred.
A leopard stalks and pounces,
Killing one off guard.
The chilly dawn is warming
Sun's up –
The river flows.
Sustaining life around it,
No matter where it goes.

May

1990

It is Africa

It fills me with a profound feeling of passion
For a land and her wildlife.
It has moved me to tears
Whilst sitting on a kopje,
Looking out over game-studded dry riverbeds.
It has provided me with heart-stopping moments
As lions kill.
It has placed cheetahs on my trail.
It has endeared me to the little creatures
Of the desert sands,
And amazed me as eagles sweep the sky.
It is a place which refreshes the soul.
It is a place where man is still very much in the minority
And where the land remains essentially
As it was originally architected
By our Creator.
It is wild.
It is free.
And it's home to so many of our beloved animals.
It knows many colours,
And survives harsh conditions.
It is my favourite game park.
It is the Kalahari National Park.

Top: Author in Botswana
Bottom: The wilderness workhorse. Namibia

Top: Warthog. Umfolozi Park, SA
Bottom: Elephant Herd. Kruger, SA

Top: Hyena Pups. Kruger, SA
Bottom: Vervet Monkeys. Kruger, SA

Top: Zebra. Hluhluwe Reserve, SA
Bottom: Rhino and Calf. Mkuze Reserve, SA

Top: Elephant and Calf. Olifants River, Kruger
Bottom: Impala Herd. Kruger Park, SA

Top left: Mokoro at sunrise. Maun, Botswana
Top right: Waterbuck Bull, Kruger, SA
Bottom left: Hiker in Drakensberg Mountains, SA
Bottom right: Victoria Falls, Zimbabwe

Top: Okavango Swamps, Botswana, from the air
Bottom: Namib Dunes

Top left: Alpha hyena with pup. Kruger Park, SA
Top right: Giraffe drinking. Hwange Park, Zimbabwe
Bottom left: Cheetah. Hluhluwe Reserve, SA
Bottom right: Crowded waterhole. Etosha, Namibia

Top: Hippo. Okavango Swamps, Botswana
Bottom: Meerkat. Kalahari, SA

Top: Kudu Ewe. Kruger Park , SA
Bottom: Mating pair of lions, Sirheni. Kruger Park, SA

Top: Jackal with its kill. Kalahari, SA
Bottom: Lion with elephant carcass. Etosha

Top: Doum Palm. Shaba Reserve, Kenya
Bottom: Leopard. Samburu Reserve, Kenya

Top: Lioness with cubs. Shingwedzi, Kruger
Bottom: Author at Elsa's grave. Meru Reserve, Kenya

Top: Saddle-billed stork with baby croc. Kruger, SA
Bottom: Zebra. Etosha, Namibia

Top left: Kay reading after scattering Marie's ashes. Weenen
Top right: Sub-adult male elephant. Phinda, SA
Bottom left: Cheetah family. Timbavati Reserve, SA
Bottom right: Gemsbok. Namib Desert, Namibia

Top: Lioness portrait. Kruger, SA
Bottom: Lioness in riverbed. Kruger, SA

I WASN'T EXPECTING IT – WE HAD ONLY left camp a few minutes beforehand. We were driving in the riverbed, and as we rounded the bend our way through was blocked by the carcass of a large male gemsbok which had been disembowelled. We had no choice but to stop.

The usual starkness of the Kalahari was awash with the golden spread of the sun's awakening rays, and apart from the intermittent chatter of the African dawn it was silent and still.

Her hot breath trickled into the cold Kalahari air whilst she guarded her kill from the riverbank to our left. *This* was life itself. A lioness in her prime, replete from her first gorging of gemsbok flesh, ever watchful, engraved against the dissemination of night. As she stood up and walked towards the gemsbok there was a sensuality about her movement, a confident and promiscuous stride which relayed itself to us, in human terms, as a very definite ownership of not only the carcass, but of the inheritance of this rich and ancient land from her terrestrial ancestors.

As she stood over the gemsbok she lifted her head, tensed every muscle in her lithe body, and with an immense effort hauled the carcass out of the riverbed and through the grass to a broken-down tree trunk about a hundred metres from where we were stopped.

Now, with the lioness virtually out of sight, we reluctantly switched on the motor and moved off, proudly appreciating that we had been alone with the lioness, and that the next car to round the bend would have no knowledge of the moving scenario which had just taken place.

AUGUST
1996

Due to a turning point in my life, 'heading off into the bush' lost some of its previous simplicity and spontaneity, and I needed some questions answered.

It was in the mountainous areas of Kwa-Zulu Natal and in the quiet rural countryside of the Natal Midlands that I sought these answers.

The poems that I wrote in these peaceful sanctuaries are dedicated to my dear friend, Marie.

QUIETLY I SPEAK

So very different
But so much the same.
A gift I've been blessed with
To help ease the pain.
From worlds apart,
A land of wild dreams,
The depths of my feelings
Is *my* song, it seems.
The words are unspoken
So much of the time,
But I know in my heart
I need this climb.
So often I wonder,
If thoughts I express
Reach out in confusion,
The tears to caress.
So happy to be, yet
So sad if it's lost,
A treasure to kindle
Whatever the cost.

64

BLIND MAN'S CORNER

T'was a four-hour walk to the corner,
A blind man named the spot.
Beneath the peak of Cathkin
Renowned as God's own plot.
And the mist hung so low that day.
From base there was no sign
Of the path that led towards it
Beyond the sphinx of time.
The forested track led secretly
Through damp and silent turns,
The beads of spider's cobwebs
Were laced between the ferns.
The incline was relentless,
It veered to grasp the contour.
The rock face ever closer,
The edge became a lure.
As I eased beyond the foggy screen
An eerie sense prevailed,
A sudden change in vista
Steel blue and sunshine hailed.
To stand and gaze in awe and glory
The peak of Cathkin proud.
Etched against a winter's sky,
No sign of morning cloud.
The final haul seemed strangely tardy,
Three Eland stopped to stare.
Baboons called out to cheer me.
I knew that I was there.

SEASONS IN THE MOUNTAINS

Summer.
Jade and cloaked in velvet
Scalloped, ever changing
Thrusting upwards
Caressed by lengthening shadows.
The Mountains of the Dragon.

Autumn.
Ochre, dipping in gold dust
Carved and never failing
Strong, foreboding
Embraced by quickening lustres
The Mountains of the Dragon.

Winter.
Amethyst and naked
Proudly set, imposing
Still and frozen
Benumbed by snowy mantles
The Mountains of the Dragon.

Spring.
Jonquil, laced with blossoms
Etched in lofty grandeur
Proud, unveiling
Blessed with champagne sequins
The Dragon's wings unfurl.

THE GORGE

Strangely shaped rocks
A gentle breeze blowing
Closer to Heaven
At first without knowing.
The world below
Past the forested slope
The Umzimkulu
Makes a journey of hope.
Down through the gorge
In a season of flood
The river rages
With the valley's life blood.
Above the scene
The eagles are riding
The thermals above
The Oribi's hiding.
Nothing has changed
In this chasm of bode
T'was carved by God's hand
When his seeds were first sown.

THE SPHINX

To be atop the mighty hill,
To look erstwhile and ponder.
To smell the air, to taste the thrill,
Imagining what's yonder.
To stand as they had done before,
To ogle over valleys.
To see the stage, to meet the men,
Imagining reveilles.
To listen to the eagles cry,
To feel the wind ablowing,
To know the heat that seared that day,
Imagining sweat flowing.
To watch the mass rise tall and wide,
To contemplate the fury,
To try and think of queen and flag,
Imagining the jury.
To muster guns and bullets too,
To forge a quickening front,
To bolster lines, and dig a trench,
Imagining some wild hunt.
To feel the terror of the clash,
To know the odds against you,
To blindly rush the closing lines,
Imagining 'Abantu'.
To bear the pain, to cup the loss,
To reminisce the laughter,
To cry aloud, to shed a tear,
Imagining hereafter.
To be atop the mighty hill,
To look erstwhile and ponder,
To walk among the young men's graves,
Legends of Isandhlwana.

AUGUST
1999

I CAN THINK OF NO BETTER PLACE IN which to surrender the ashes of a loved one. From an elevated kopje which overlooked an expanse of remarkably beautiful bushveld, we watched the tired sun set. It scorched the horizon before it slipped into the abyss below, and it was then that these final, yet blessed remnants of life were released. They were gently carried away by a lingering flow of warm air, to be dispersed and returned to the Earth.

Marie and I accompanied our friend Ian, and we had travelled a long way to perform this sacred rite. Itala Game Reserve is a special place, hidden away in the mountainous area of northern Zululand. It is exceptionally scenic, with a distinctly unique atmosphere. It is spiritually encapsulating, and is one of those rare places where the remoteness and mountainous contours, versus deeply cut gorges and valleys, suffices, and therefore encountering any game is a bonus and by no means a necessity.

During off-peak periods the narrow and intriguing network of gravel roads is free of man and his vehicle, and due to the lack of major predators one is allowed to stroll within a five-metre radius of one's car anywhere in the reserve. This facilitates the exploration of interesting nooks, and contemplation of spoor, feathers, droppings and other signs of the wild.

In this secluded haven I was not at all surprised to be made aware of the fact that 'Dung Beetles have right of way'. All the animals that I came across in the park seemed relaxed and unconcerned at my presence, so I was able to acquire some classic photographic material with relative ease. The unusual backdrop of undulating reserve endowed simple sightings with photogenic and enhanced countenance. This was a place of pure magic, where at every turn a new and inspiring vista ensued.

As I drove down a steep incline and into a river crossing my concentration almost cost me the sighting of an enormous white rhino and her calf drinking from an ephemeral pool of water. Towering sycamore fig trees, the Pongola River carving its way through the valley floor and bald ibis hugging the rock face surrounding the camp at Ntshondwe are images indelibly etched in my mind, and I want to return – next time in the summer months, when the gold and purple landscape of winter will be transformed into green.

SANCTUS

As the candle flickers, it gently glows,
Silent words, that no one else knows.
Caressing the heart
With gossamer strings,
I feel torn apart
By the peace this all brings.

DOES THE ROBIN STILL CALL IN AFRICA?

Does the robin still call in Africa?

"Oh yes"

How do you know?

"I've heard him"

When did you last hear him?

"This morning"

Where?

"In my garden"

It must have been a fleeting glimpse?

"Not at all. He and his mate live here.

I've watched him build a nest in the ivy,

Just outside the kitchen window,

I provide water for him to bathe twice a day.

We sing to each other.

I rescued him when he strayed from his flight path

And became disorientated in the lounge of my home,

And I shared in his joy

When he announced the arrival of his offspring."

You are privileged.

"I know."

THE YEAR
2000

M ARIE'S AND MY JOURNEYS INTO THE WILD places of Africa recommenced. A return to the magical world of 'heading off into the bush', which had existed prior to Marie's illness in 1996, began again. Whilst in camp one night, deep in the Kruger National Park, I continued with entries in my 'journal of sublime moments'.

The Collins Dictionary definition of 'sublime' is: *Something inspiring deep veneration, awe or uplifting emotion because of its beauty, nobility, grandeur or immensity.*

I considered one of my favourite pieces of poetry:

The Art of Living
Anonymous

To touch the cup with eager lips, and taste, not drain it;
To woo, and tempt, and count a bliss, and not attain it;
To fondle and caress a Joy, yet hold it lightly,
Lest it become necessity and cling too tightly;
To watch the sunset in the west without regretting;
To hail its advent in the east, the night forgetting.
To smother care in happiness, and grief in laughter;
To hold the present close, not questioning the hereafter;
To have enough to share, to know the Joy of giving;
To thrill with all the sweets of life – that's living

May

2000

SATARA CAMP

THE WINTER'S NIGHT HAD FALLEN EARLY.

I began to meditate on the manner in which the wilderness affects some people. Perhaps we share some kind of inherited memory gene. It's almost the opposite of reality. There is a deep yearning to return to the natural freedom of an uncultivated state of being. In fact I have often deliberated on this very issue. Is reality our everyday humdrum lifestyle, or is it that of returning to our roots? Over the glowing coals which had chargrilled the steaks, a glass of red wine seemed to divine my thoughts towards the mulling over of life's web of existence.

After some time of quiet contemplation the metropolis of stars above began slowly disappearing behind a veil of haze. A broadening blush of crimson was painting the dark sky in the east. After observing the phenomenon and its expanding range, it became clear that this was a fire raging through the bush. I recall dwelling on the fire's ferocity within its localised area and of the terrible loss, not only of life, but of habitat as well.

As the dry months draw in this is always one of the favourable trials of life. New shoots of grass push through the burnt earth, which in turn benefit the new offspring appearing around September. In the meantime, however, I mused over the tortoises, too slow to escape the flames, the snakes unable to hide, the infirm and the lost. The wilderness is a place of extreme survival. Survival of the fittest. Sentimentality has no real place in the African savannah, but that is what makes humans different. Our thoughts and our imagination.

It was sixteen wild dog puppies in the road, soaking in the warmth of the early morning sun, that finally eradicated the dreadful thoughts of the previous night's events. The adults were on the verge, supervising this torrent of canine adventure. An approaching vehicle stopped alongside mine; it was a conservation ranger.

His words were gabbled excitedly, "You will never see anything like this ever again."
To this day, I never have.

Gratitude is the memory of the heart.

Johann Wolfgang von Goethe.

PRETORIUSKOP
KRUGER PARK

IT WAS ONE OF THOSE DAYS WHICH I had come to recognise. I accepted my subservience to Africa's spell. It had done me no harm. In fact it had prepared me for a dimension which I am certain is to follow. I have never been able to come to terms with the moment when I have had to leave the respite of a game reserve. The onslaught of city life means returning to the conformity of schedules, restrictions, noise, crowds, pollution and demands. Somehow on these days I have found it difficult to peer into the surrounding rhapsody of a natural world. This is because I have known that if I have spotted something just a little different, I would want to stay.

On that morning, the light of day was encroaching into the night. Unexpectedly, and as he crossed the road, a large male leopard was caught in the beam of the dimmed headlights. By the time I was able to ascertain exactly where he had left the road and gone into the bush, he was just visible walking along the riverbed below me.

As dawn broke, my eyes seemed to reflect eternity. Shafts of light gleamed upon the white tip of the leopard's tail as he trod the ancient dry sand of a previously full and flowing river. Visuals were poor without binoculars, but as I looked through them the leopard's lithe body filled the lens. During his climb from the river floor, over rocks and boulders, I followed him. I had only intermittent sightings of this large cat, as he climbed the steep kopje (hillside). Mindful of a leopard's nocturnal lifestyle, he was probably returning to his lair after a night's hunt. Through my field glasses I searched the summit of the kopje. There were some huge rocks, naked against the youthfully muted morning sky. Time then elapsed.

Having not sighted the leopard in the thick undergrowth for over half an hour I decided it was time to leave. Unable to resist one final look through my binoculars, this great African continent once again endowed me with yet another heart-stopping moment. The leopard had reached the summit. There he stretched, lay down, and

74

draped his paws over the rock's edge. Holding his head high it was evident that this was his domain, and the view from his throne reached out over the vast expanse of Africa.

As the sun moved a little higher the leopard reclined. It was time for him to enjoy the warmth of the fast-approaching day.

For me, the whole earth was in repose.

Quote:
There is a relationship between the health of the human spirit, and the health of the last vestiges of the wilderness.

John Varty

MAY

2002

TIMBAVATI GAME RESERVE

M Y NEPHEW SIMON, ON HOLIDAY FROM ENGLAND, was with me. In celebration of his twenty-eighth birthday he wanted to see the 'Big Five' (this is a term given to the sighting of lion, leopard, elephant, rhino and buffalo in the wild). He had already decided that his trophy of achievement to be taken back to England would be a hand-painted ostrich egg depicting the Big Five.

In commemoration of my nephew's first visit to Africa I wanted to see cheetah cubs, one of the few sightings which had eluded me in Africa. It was our second to last day in the reserve. The sun was up, and the dewy cobwebs still spanned the space between the tall grasses. These trusting strands were left in tatters, betrayed by the movement of the Land Rover, responding to a crackling message over the driver's radio. A cheetah with cubs had been spotted just a few kilometres away and they were walking down a gravel track. My chest tightened, and my eyes met those of Simon. At this moment I was as excited as I had been in 1976, when I had experienced my first game drive.

Slowly emerging from the dense bush we turned onto the track and there, no more than twenty metres away, was an adult female cheetah with her three small cubs. They all sat down. The cheetah cubs were fluffy and wrapped in their black capes, nature's mantle of camouflage resembling the fur of a ratel or honey badger. Silently, tears ran the gauntlet of my cheeks. This was a magical and unique experience for me. After almost thirty years of driving in the African reserves, I now had the four of them in the eye of my camera, and even more preciously, etched in my memory forever.

A knowing hug from my nephew completed this fleeting moment in time.

Quote:
Collect these moments to remember life's Joys.

Unknown

THE NEXT DAY

"SIMON, QUICKLY, GET UP!" THIS WAS OUR last day in the Timbavati area. My nephew still had to see one more animal in order to clinch his ostrich egg. "Simon, I can hear lion!" This was what he needed.

Within moments we were at the Land Rover, ready to go. It was still dark. The ranger and tracker appeared from nowhere with their guns required as protection. The engine was started. Again the lion roared! Once we had bumped our way over the rugged road and onto a sandy track the lion spoor was easy to track, and with the currently intermittent but regular roar of the lion it wasn't too difficult for the tracker to do his job.

The darkness still surrounded us when we first spotted him; a beautifully black-maned lion, of enormous proportions. This time it was Simon's heart that almost ceased to beat.

As the sun commenced its steep upward journey, heralding yet another glorious day in the African bush, I pondered the emotive tug which I perceived to be exploding within my nephew. He could now rightfully claim his ostrich egg, and I was able to claim a soulmate. Simon, too, was in love with Africa!

Sometime afterwards, whilst returning to camp for breakfast, in the distance we could see an animal walking towards us. Still deep in the bush, the driver stopped the engine. We didn't have to wait long to realise that it was the lion that we had previously been watching. He had walked a circuitous route which had brought him back into our path. The lion's purposeful stride in the direction of our vehicle portrayed a demeanour that he was 'on a mission'. As he came within about forty metres of the Land Rover he began to roar; a roar which disseminated from the throat of a powerful monarch. Vibrations resonated in the crisp morning air and as the lion reached the vehicle he stopped and looked directly at Simon. His roaring seemed more vital now, as his mouth strained to emit his vocal urgency.

As George Adamson's cook, Korokoro, interpreted all those years ago in the Meru National Park in Kenya, the roar of the African lion is reaffirming, for all to hear…

"Who is lord of the land…? Who is lord of the land…? I am… I am… I am."

SEPTEMBER

2002

SHINGWEDZI CAMP,
KRUGER

WE STOPPED THE CAMPERVAN BENEATH A LARGE mahogany tree. It was hot, and although just a few kilometres from camp I sensed there might be something in the riverbed over which I now glanced. As so often happened when acting on my instincts I could hardly believe my eyes.

There, in the parched riverbed, was a most beautiful lioness. She proudly lay in the sand, her dignity and feline power uppermost in the mind of any creature that might stumble into or indeed encroach upon her riverine territory. I had heard talk of a group of lionesses living close to the camp. Apparently there were three cubs with the maternal lioness, and as usual, her 'aunts' who were there to attend to the mother's needs and to assist in bringing her prey.

I opened the sliding roof of the vehicle and with the aid of binoculars scanned the riverine floor for signs of any other leonine life. Just as a second sleeping lioness slipped into my view there was a noise above my head. Before I had a chance to look up a juvenile leopard dropped from the cover of the tree and landed on the sandy track in front of me, missing the front bumper by less than a single metre!

Never before in all my years in the African wilderness had I encountered such a narrow escape, but at the same time been part of such an encounter! From that day onwards, whenever I squeezed myself through the sliding roof, I never failed to look upwards! The lioness remained in her regal pose, whilst the leopard ambled down the trail, until he veered off into the dense bush.

PRETORIUSKOP,
KRUGER PARK

THE JOY OF BEING IMMERSED IN NATURE is that it promotes an outpouring of gentleness in character.

Early morning on the road was the best time for viewing game, prior to the unrelenting heat of an African day becoming perceptible. I was slowly travelling the road, as a wildlife photographer's instincts dictate. For some reason I suggested that we stop. I turned down the window and inhaled the sweetly scented aromas of the African bush. I will never know what it was that made me come to a halt.

Within moments a lioness emerged from the ditch below the road. As she sat on the verge directly in front of me I could see that she was slightly agitated. She looked behind her. There was an absolute, indescribable silence. She stood up; then, heaving their little bodies up onto the edge of the roadside alongside her, came three tiny cubs.

I had been exposed to so many encapsulating moments over the many years I had spent in the bush, but this was a sight so far unsurpassed. My vision was blurred. This was a tender moment. Maternal instinct was at its height. The lioness looked at my vehicle, and then in both directions of the road. She clearly wanted to cross. The cubs, who could not have been more than twelve weeks old, obediently sat by their mother. The lioness reclined again. In the golden light of early dawn the family was in no hurry. I was instantly aware that this was one of those moments that could never be erased from my memory.

A deep-throated roar shattered the peaceful calm. The lioness stood up, a stance quickly adopted by the cubs, and she walked to the centre of the road; the grip on my slippery hands tightened. She turned to her cubs, and they followed. Together they gambolled off into the bush on the opposite side of the road towards the direction of the roar. They were gone, as if they had never been there.

May
2003

KENYA, EAST AFRICA

O NE OF THE FINEST DAYS OF MY life.

I had flown in from Johannesburg the day before. The driver collected me from my Nairobi hotel and together we drove to Elsamere (Joy Adamson's home) on the edge of Lake Naivasha in the Rift Valley.

Keeping to the potholed road as far as the escarpment edge I looked down into the sculpted valley. For nearly forty years I had been 'homesick' for a place I had never seen. For almost as long as I could remember I was 'going to Africa'. I had visualised sun-drenched plains supporting a myriad of wild creatures. I had tried to imagine the quintessential lifestyle of living in a tent by a river with a fully grown lioness. An unimaginable sensation of balm soothed the very core of my being.

We continued on the deteriorating roads, until suddenly Lake Naivasha and Elsamere announced themselves. I was speechless, and unable to stem the ceaseless flow of tears, which spilled over and travelled downwards in a steady stream. I had arrived.

This was a special place, one of unrelenting beauty, the grounds, the trees, the flowers and the lake all emitting their own exquisite portion of perfection. There seemed to be birds everywhere, and colobus monkeys, surely descendants of the ones whom Joy herself had cherished. I was able to discern a strong sense of spirit in this secluded corner of Kenya. The life force of Joy, George and lions permeated the atmosphere. The essence of Penny remained here too. Penny, a wild leopard cub, had lived at Elsamere for some months before Joy had been able to release her into the wild territory of Shaba Reserve, close to that of Meru.

Returning to Nairobi that evening, I left behind a paradise such as I had never known, and remote as the possibility seemed, I somehow knew that I would be back one day.

JUNE 1ST
2003

MERU NATIONAL PARK

Quote:

*We are the wanderers of this earth. Our hearts are full of wonder, and
our souls are full of dreams.*

Unknown

MY CHARTER FLIGHT TOOK ME ON A route from Nairobi over the Rift Valley and into the reserve. From the air Mugwango Hill rose up from the swamplands and flat grassy plains of Meru. My luxury cave set deeply within this hillside looked down over the last traces of George Adamson's spartan camp. It was perfectly placed between doum palms and acacia trees. I began to feel that I was now being drawn into a genuine African legend. A story that was inspiring an intense and ethereal longing within me. It was a journey into a wilderness that evoked a deep-rooted anticipation. It was an experience that was enriching the crux of my being with a flood of memories. Memories from a dimension of which I had no conscious recollection. I knew nothing of their origin. I seemed to be walking in the footsteps of my ancestors, yet feeling totally at home in surroundings of comfort and style.

Although my burning desire was to find Elsa's grave I took the opportunity to walk through George's camp with an armed ranger, as protection from the many wild animals that roamed the reserve. To walk in the footsteps of such a wise stalwart of lion knowledge was not only unbearably meaningful for me, but overwhelming from an emotional and mystical perspective. I could not believe how fortunate I was. There were no words to describe this overwhelming sense of grace.

81

During the first game drive we drove past one of George's favourite spots on the bank of the Rojewero River. It was beneath a huge fig tree that he used to fish with his lions beside him.

As Grant's gazelle, reticulated giraffe and lesser kudu looked on we drank sundowners whilst we gazed out on the setting sun which was dipping below the Nyambeni Mountains. Being so close to the equator sunset was over in a brief interval, but despite this the air remained warm and thick. Back at camp I listened to hyenas howling and laughing at the night's events, and there was lots of talk of elephant that had been wandering around the area of George's camp, where I had been that morning. There were snake stories too, including sightings around the lodge. I felt very adventurous knowing that I had opted to have no closed frontage to my 'cave'.

By 22.00hrs I was listening to the utter absence of noise, barring the occasional wild sound of night creatures. There were millions of stars above me. From the midst of this luxurious setting my thoughts were simple. "The Adamsons were so brave, and I am so privileged." Being afraid had never been further from my mind. My soul was content… Elsa's spirit was with me. I slept.

Quote:

I was never less alone than by myself.

Edward Gibbon

JUNE 2ND
2003

I AWOKE AT 05.30HRS AND SUNRISE LASTED ABOUT half a minute. Today, George (my driver) and I travelled to the Tana River, which is the longest river in Kenya. We also found the Adamson's Falls, which were discovered by George Adamson himself. I had breakfast here overlooking these ferocious falls, which were amazingly wild and beautiful. Vulturine guineafowl, orange-bellied parrots and yellow-necked spurfowl either strutted around the area or called from their perches.

On the way back to camp my driver took me to visit Pippa's grave and the grave of one of her cubs, so lovingly close to each other. Pippa was the cheetah that Joy rehabilitated back into the wild. As I ran my fingers through the grasses that swayed around the grave I reflected on the days of my youth when I had read Joy's book, *Pippa's Challenge*.

Back at camp that night I mentally prepared myself for the next day and the purpose of my mission. The visit to Elsa's grave.

JUNE 3RD
2003

B Y 05.00HRS I COULD SEE VENUS AND one other small star from my bed. Moments afterwards, and from my deck, I could hear elephants breaking branches. With the appearance of the sun there was a fracas amongst a troop of baboons that were close by, and rocks emerged as elephants. This was a living Eden, and I was part of it!

Today was to be the realisation of my childhood dream

Elsa's Camp by the River Ura was wild, remote, secretive and overgrown. The grave was close by. It was at this camp where Joy used to paint and write, with Elsa at her side. I felt an unbelievable sense of awareness, almost expecting to see Joy, George, and Elsa. I looked up at Elsa's Rock, the rock on which she used to love to laze. I was living history.

We arrived at the grave. I was unashamedly emotional.

What an honour to be here. This was the place where Elsa had brought her tiny cubs across the river to meet Joy and George, the place that millions of people around the world had read about. But a place which so few people had visited. Obviously Joy, George and Elsa's cubs, Jespah, Gopa and little Elsa, had been here. But they were all dead. There was only one person whom I knew of that had been taken here by Joy herself, and who was indeed still alive. This was the actress who had played the part of Joy Adamson in the movie *Born Free*. Her name – Virginia McKenna.

Before George (my driver) took the Land Rover to a spot where he could discreetly disappear, a manoeuvre which ensured my privacy at the grave, he did something for me. I had been given permission by management staff at the lodge to bury the collars of my dogs, Elsa, Jespah and Gopa beside the grave. George dug a hole to facilitate this. I felt that a part of my beloved dogs could be with their namesake. I prayed to St Francis to look after the animals of the world. I then had the day to myself under a large acacia tree, where I wrote down my thoughts and thanked God for it all. Whilst I nibbled on food from the beautiful picnic that the manageress had prepared for me I opened the envelope that she had given to me. I had been asked to promise that I wouldn't open it until I was at Elsa's grave.

It was a card, and on the front was a picture of George Adamson and Elsa on top of Elsa's Rock. Inside were the words of E. E. Cummings.

"How fortunate are you and I,
Whose home is timeless. We who
Have wandered down from the
Fragrance of eternal now

To frolic in such timeless
Mysteries as birth and death, a
Day, (or maybe even less)"

I was overpowered by something that I didn't fully comprehend.

Whilst at the grave I wrote. I didn't have to think. My hand followed the pen.

~ I am sitting at Elsa's grave '1956 -1961' ~

I will never be able to express how I feel.

I feel that I am completely at peace at last, and where I should be, close to the spirit of Elsa, who has been the guiding force in my life. It is so secretive here, abounding with lush riverine vegetation, palms, grasses and acacias. The River Ura is running behind Elsa's grave.

Joy is also here with Elsa. Well, half here and half with Pippa the cheetah.

This location is hidden away so deeply in the Kenyan bush – Meru – and so close to Elsa's Camp, from where Joy and George had released Elsa back into the wild.

There is no one here, hardly visible vehicle strips, birds singing; and now the collars of my beloved dogs, Elsa's namesakes, are with her.

How lucky am I to have belonged to Meru for a brief moment in time; how rich I am... I don't know what I did to earn the grace of this privilege, save the acceptance of the gift of faith, and the resolve to discover an affinity with nature and its entire offspring.

It is no coincidence that I am here; I know it is my destiny. Perhaps there is something in my life still to come that I don't know about.

What I do know, however, is that this is an experience that has touched me deeply... so deeply that only a very few people would ever be able to understand the depth of love and warmth in my soul from being in Elsa's Africa.

I remember reading somewhere that only those who are ready and seeking will normally understand. My own thoughts led me here, but it would not have been possible without my belief in God which has enriched this experience. I believe strongly that there is a communion of saints, and that the spirits of Elsa (and other creatures) have indeed met and worked through humankind, which has in turn guided their actions and destiny.

I will always love the memory of Elsa and her cubs, Jespah, Gopa and little Elsa, admire the memories of Joy and George Adamson, but I will always love Meru, because I have met it. Meru endowed me with the miracle of fulfilling my lifetime's dream.

I am not afraid here. There is a great peace that comes with silence.

There is almost every species of East African game roaming freely here, and yet I feel safe and content in my soul, praying that somehow the continuation and the preservation of all wildlife and its habitat will continue.

On return to camp I spent some time at the camp's lookout, which is where the sun can be glanced, slipping behind the Nyambeni hills. A fire was lit and after a glass of wine, alone with my thoughts, I was joined by the manageress. I told her that although I hadn't seen a lion whilst in Meru I would have been content just to have heard one! We chatted until dark, when she had to leave. I was left with a sky full of stars, a new moon, a fire and a glass of wine. I unhurriedly enjoyed my final dinner privately on the deck that night, to the sound of hyenas' laughing. I was in love with Meru and I didn't go to sleep until 23.00hrs, after once again trying to put my love affair into print.

On that night, I felt that I was, indeed, seated very close to *Nkulunkulu* (great creator spirit).

86

JUNE 4ST
2003

TODAY I HAD TO SAY GOODBYE TO Meru.

At 05.30hrs I was on my deck looking out into the last moments of the African night. And then... in the far distance I heard the whuffing of lions. Was I dreaming? No! In the next half an hour I heard them three more times! I estimated that the sounds were coming from about five kilometres away, certainly from within the vicinity of Elsa's previous territory.

Elsa had not let me down. I felt exhilarated.

I pondered over the fact that I did not have a puppy named little Elsa. I became convinced that one day, even though I had four dogs, and no desire for a fifth, a little Elsa would take up her rightful place with me... *and if I were to have just one more miracle it would be to return to Meru in order to bury her collar, along with those of her sisters and her spiritual guardian, Elsa the lioness.*

I fully understood that the chance of that happening was indeed remote, if not impossible.

Soon after this there came a knock on my door. It was time to go to the airstrip. I was to return to Nairobi and then to South Africa. It was so hard to get into that little plane. George handed me a small gift from the management team. It was a beaded Taraka dancing skirt. I couldn't speak, not even to say goodbye.

The engines started up and we began our race along the strip.

Sad, sad, sad as the red earth fell away beneath me, but utterly complete within my heart. Goodbye Meru. Will we ever meet again?

JUNE
2004

NIGHT-TIME,
PHINDA GAME RESERVE,
MKUZE

I T HAD BEEN A REWARDING GAME DRIVE in an open Land Rover. I had delighted in the countless eyes reflected in the headlights. So many in fact, that they appeared almost like stars in the night sky. The eyes belonged mostly to impala, but there were also zebra and wildebeest staring back at me. I had spotted a bushbaby in the upper reaches of a fruiting tree, hugging a tiny youngster to her chest. It seemed appropriate that the nightjar sang his never ending song of "good lord deliver us".

The watery ponds, although unseen in the wintery night, were crowded. Frogs of unlimited varieties whistled and croaked in a never-ending cacophony of resonating sounds. I remembered something that I had read once.

It was about 'never being alone, and being able to claim kinship with everything'. Again I mused over the mystery of creation. Who or what is in charge of all this? I pondered over global warming. Not everyone was taking it seriously.

It seemed strange to visualise a polar bear hanging on to a chunk of floating ice in the Arctic, whilst I was enjoying a balmy African night. But there was no difference really. I tried to imagine a silent world. With that thought came a unique African sound. It was unmistakable and it sent a signal of trepidation into my primitive DNA.

On a narrow strip of road a lion lay camouflaged in the tall grass. The ranger stopped no more than five metres away from this magnificent creature. The infrared tracking device then illuminated a second heavily maned lion. We were frighteningly close.

Very quietly we sat in the dense blackness of the night, exposed, yet bound by an ancient thread. Silence, save for my own heartbeat pounding in my ears.

With the infrared turned off I could see nothing through the small space which separated us. And then simultaneously both the lions roared into this night of an echoing distant past. I had never heard any sound so penetrating. A crescendo of deep guttural roars seemed to vibrate its way into the fountainhead of my soul. This was not a time of fear for me. It was something on the outer edge of reality which was blending with an earthly, yet spiritual state of awe. Again I tried to imagine a silent world.

SEPTEMBER
2004

KWA-ZULU NATAL

04.00HRS. IT WAS DARK AND A LITTLE chilly. The Hluhluwe/Umfolozi Game Reserves were beckoning. These parks, no more than a two-and–a-half hour drive from Durban, are tucked away between the scalloped hills and valleys of northern Kwa-Zulu Natal. I needed a break, and Marie came along with me.

Leaving Durban, still sleepy in the velvety night, had an uplifting familiarity which never failed to evoke an impression of adventure. At this hour it was easy to visualise our planet as if it were a crown in the universe, a crown where all living species were depicted as the jewels; a kind of galaxy which had spread out since the time of Noah's Ark. I often considered the very real possibility of this jewelled tiara becoming a crown of thorns.

Travelling to a well-loved destination always opened the window of my soul a little wider than usual. The sky was all around, and its shifting moods and colours created an artistic 'pie in the sky'.

There was a crocodile in the midst of a glowing inferno of dust, and a perfectly silhouetted sycamore fig tree adorned in its new foliage, providing disguise to what could have been the long neck of a giraffe.

A very short distance from the entrance to the reserve there was movement ahead of us, towards the side of the road. There were no houses, domestic livestock or other vehicles on the narrow route, and it was now light enough to see with clarity. With an abrupt urgency and no more than a hundred metres in front of our oncoming car a man left the verge side and tumbled into the road. As I braked he started waving as if to slow us down. He then turned to face us with legs spread wide apart.

At fifty metres he drew his pistol, and on this lonely stretch of rural Africa, pointed it at the windscreen. I now became aware that when faced with impending death two differing areas of the brain work together in perfect unison. Firstly the rapid catalogue of my life's events raced into my conscious mind. Secondly, being familiar with nursing

90

traumatised patients in an intensive care environment, I recalled the injuries inflicted on innocent victims in situations such as these. I thought of the Adamsons' violent deaths in Kenya, and I wondered what horrors lay ahead for us too. Here and now was no time for prayer, but I do remember calling out "Oh God!"

With that, my 'other brain', well trained to deal with emergencies, took over.

The road ahead was straight; I put my hand on Marie's head and pushed down hard. "Get under the dashboard!" I yelled.

I too, firmly gripping the steering wheel, ducked below the windscreen and depressed the accelerator. I couldn't stay down for long, and I was thankful that so far we hadn't hit anything in the road. My decision to take over full visual control of the car was made for me, when a loud, resonating "Bang" from the shot fired at us from behind brought me to my senses. We had escaped unscathed and continued the rest of our journey in silent disbelief.

Man is such a problem.

It was following this incident that I faced up to the reality of 'life after death'. Indeed, more specifically, 'life on planet earth, after my death'. I recalled so many anecdotes about individual contributions, and I can relate my personal need towards leaving a legacy to this event.

Quote:
There is no point in discovering, if there is no contribution.
Unknown

On that day in September 2004, I entered the game reserve a different person. It was as if I had crossed some kind of threshold. Nothing seemed quite the same. I was somehow detached. In the surreal aftermath of a 'life-threatening experience' I became aware that the moving grey battleships I now gazed upon were real, live elephants. A large herd of elephants; a matriarch, young adults, teenagers and tiny ones, some so small that they were hardly able to reach the teats of their mother in order to drink.

Whether I were alive or dead, it was an incomprehensible thought that these living giants would not continue to wander the plains of Africa, their survival so dependent on man. So many words are written about leaving the world a better place for our children. Well yes, I agree, but what about the elephants? Don't they deserve a better place?

My life changed on that day.

St Thomas Aquinas, in his Summa Theologica
Admits the right of belief that animals have souls.

May
2005

Northern Kruger

T HE EVENING STAR, VENUS, WAS PROUDLY REFLECTED in the watercourse in front of the camp. Filtering through the cool night air came the typical descending wail of the water dikkop speaking of its plight. The fiery-necked nightjar simultaneously identified itself, piping, "Good lord deliver us".

I continued to discover dormant forces within the core of my being. This hushed collection of flowing perception was the secret to happiness. From the beginning of the birth of my wisdom, deep in the wilderness of Africa, I realised that discovery of 'self' never ends. My thoughts went back to those teenage dreams of mine in the 1960s.

The trouble with choosing to *live* in Africa is that our footprints become different somehow. We go to different places and we notice a diversity of existence. Nature instructs us almost everywhere. Courage and endurance *is* the bird that perches in the soul, and hangs on despite adversity.

As I looked up at another perfectly rounded African moon it didn't seem possible that man had landed on this celestial body. But then neither did it seem possible that on one night a lioness had mated with a wild lion, deep in the African bush of Meru, and on the next had slept soundly close to her human 'parents' in a tent.

Quote:
Do not go where the path may lead, go instead where there is no path and leave a trail.

Ralph Waldo Emerson

NORTHERN KRUGER

THE BRANCHES IN THE HUGE JACKAL BERRY tree close to our hut were moving. I didn't have to use binoculars in order to discern the reason. Contentedly nibbling berries in the highest branches of the tree was a large male baboon. I was awash with 'joie de vivre'. I pondered as to why I was so utterly fulfilled in situations such as these. I reflected on the hills of Yorkshire, my late father, and life's mysteries.

An intense explosion shattered the silence of my blissful reminiscing and for a split second I was numb. And then, my beautiful baboon hit the ground with a thud. Dead. A ranger had shot him. "A potential threat to the camp residents," he said.

"What threat?" I thought. "Wasn't this what we had all come to enjoy?"

I am still haunted by this memory.

The novelist Edward Hoagland once wrote:
'We become tourists to find out how it was before we lost ourselves in the suburbs, to meet people who still own their lives and believe.'

FEBRUARY
2006

MATETSI,
ZIMBABWE

I NAMED THE ZAMBEZI RIVER 'THE RIVER OF hope'. In a country where the natural resources have been raped and neglected for years there seemed to be a ray of hope among groups of Zimbabweans whose concern for the country's wildlife seemed paramount.

When I arrived at Victoria Falls Airport I met Peter, a Zimbabwean of European descent. Having some insight into the political turmoil of this forlorn nation I instinctively enquired, "Do you have a farm?" His reply: "I *had* a farm."

This reminded me of the Dane, Karen Blixen, and her epic autobiography *Out of Africa*, which begins with the haunting line, "I had a farm in Africa, at the foot of the Ngong Hills."

Peter and Karen had lost their farms for entirely different reasons, and my heart bled for both of them. Whether one loses a farm due to land redistribution or because of failing coffee crops the wrench must be comparable. Nevertheless, Peter told me that he had hope for the future in his newly found vision for tourism. This irony of Africa in all its pristine and impenetrable harshness demonstrated its mortal and spiritual healing ability.

After arriving at Matetsi I was shown to my chalet. I was hot and dusty from the journey so I almost fell into the plunge pool. It didn't take me long to realise that I was sharing this with two monitor lizards, some frogs and a fairly sizeable troop of baboons. They seemed to prefer my pool to the waters of the Zambezi River which ran its course just in front of my dwelling. The river was full, full from the rains up in the Congo, and its journey would take it rushing over the escarpment edge to shape the Victoria Falls. I

94

was serenaded by emerald-spotted wood doves, Heuglin's robins, kingfishers, warblers, Meyer's parrots, and countless other bird species.

Each morning the sun rose quietly above the Zambezi, silhouetting trees, broken stumps and the odd hippo surfacing to catch the early morning delicacy of the crisply scented African dawn. This was a destination where it was easy to perceive a country where so many human beings were so much worse off than their average South African counterparts. From within a ravaged Zimbabwe I watched lone Zambians crossing the Zambezi River in dugout canoes, their goal to poach game from the decimated numbers that were left in Zimbabwe. Profound relativity seemed to prevail, hope being the driving force.

Fear doesn't eliminate hope. I came here to walk with lions, which unquestionably made me aware of my frailty. Canoeing the Zambezi, a river infested with hippos and crocodiles, scared me too. But I came here to test my faith in an environment of self-building. If I were able to endure this workout of the soul then my vision for the future would be fulfilled.

After walking with two thirteen-month-old lions I felt humbled. This experience had been fundamentally crucial to me. As I walked beside these regal big cats my most dormant thoughts were awakened. As if by some miracle, these thoughts were being released from captivity. It was as if there had been a transference of a primeval strength and courage. I realised this was impossible to analyse, but I seemed to fear nothing. This was the redemptive spirit of nature that I had come to know. I was in effect walking with Elsa and gaining strength from her. It was a strength about which I had no knowledge and yet, unknowingly, it would soon be needed.

Since that time I have always known that I am capable of facing any challenge.

As I sat in the timeless Africa of old I watched the waters rush past my deck, and marvelled at the trees, stoical in their stance.

After sundown and as the night deepened I looked up at a trillion stars. I gained inspiration as I mused upon all those who had gone before me. They too must have stared at the heavenly lights. Wasn't this David Livingstone's territory?

My last morning at Matetsi was heralded by birdsong. As I stepped out onto the deck, there, in my pool, was a small brown mouse swimming frantically in circles, unable to save himself. Hope of rescue must have kept him motivated until the sun rose and I stepped out onto the deck. As I scooped him out of the water, he squeaked joyfully, ran, stopped, turned around, looked at me, and then scampered into the tall grass.

Can a mouse have hope?

I like to think so.

May
2006

MY WORLD HAS BEEN TURNED UPSIDE DOWN. I experienced a personal earthquake which had crushed my self-esteem and shattered my confidence. I was seemingly adrift. I struggled to make sense of my world and I needed to rebuild my poise and conviction before my outer facade became noticeable to those who relied on my strength and ability.

Fortunately, in one brief moment, I knew the time had come, and I quickly realised that a special friend was needed. This friend would not only encourage me to revisit my personal intentions, but also to look again at my dreams and aspirations.

I reflected on my time in Meru National Park. Not only did I realise that one day there would be a time when the *Born Free* saga would, in my mind, reach its completion and I would hold a third cub 'little Elsa' in my arms. I remembered that I had actually spoken to Elsa the lioness in the repose of her grave. I had asked her to help me to discern the time for a fifth puppy. I prayed to Elsa, that somehow she would acknowledge my plea. I then remembered that I heard the distinct 'whuffing' of a lion from my balcony in Meru, not once but three times. I recalled the sheer joy that I had experienced on that morning, and the belief in my mission.

I wanted another Labrador puppy, as Jespah, my black lab, played a pivotal role in my existence. An animal action custodian was contacted. It seemed fitting that I would be rescuing the lost soul of a puppy and returning it to a loving home.

I was met by a lady of conscience who lived in a large, beautiful home. I was shown the new litter of puppies, all in need of stability and love. I looked at them. How would I choose one? I called, "Little Elsa." Something extraordinary became apparent.

Whilst peeking over a fence put in place to prevent older dogs mingling with the new recruits there befell a quiet whimpering. I looked up and saw a small crossbreed straining to show its face over the fence and, at the same time, stretching in order to secure a glance from me in its direction. I turned to the custodian and asked her if this little dog belonged to herself. She replied in the negative, and proceeded to tell me that she (it was a girl!!) and her two sisters had been abused as puppies and taken away from

96

the owner. The two sisters had gone to loving homes, but because the third pup had a 'wonky' eye she had not been chosen for a new life. My heartfelt emotions took over.

I went to the young dog, picked her up, and holding her face close to mine asked her: "Would you like to be a Little Elsa and come home with me?" My face was licked in an urgent manner. That was it. Little Elsa had been born into my world, and she had a job to do. She was about to become my mentor.

A little dog with a huge heart was all that I needed.

JANUARY 13TH

2007

AT HOME

A FTER SUPPER ONE EVENING I HAD BEEN reading the autobiography of Karen Blixen. Rain started to fall; slow large drops, chased by a torrential summer deluge. A sudden crack of thunder sparked that familiar electrical charge in the atmosphere. The thickened air spelt the anticipation of a fierce storm.

Following the toppling of a huge bougainvillea tree outside our property which had been precipitated by a violent lightning strike I put my book down. After peering through the window I chuckled to myself, *"I now have a home upon a hill which glimpses rural Africa."*

September
2008

Gqoyeni Camp,
Umfolozi Game Reserve,
Kwa-Zulu Natal

Ask and it shall be given unto you
Seek and ye shall find

Matthew 7:7

AFTER ALL MY TRAVELS IN AFRICA I found Gqoyeni to be an oasis brimming with the natural peace I had come to long for, a stillness that indeed sustained me.

Deep in the quietude of Umfolozi, this slip of Africa remained untouched by the upheaval of encroaching greed. It allowed an escape into the wealth of a profound kingdom amidst a lost Eden; surroundings where the ambience of an old-world setting could be sipped at leisure and held closely in the anticipation of possibility, a place that was able to assuage the restless spirit. Its charm was graced by an inaccessible silence.

The camp, perched on an elevation, overlooked the dry riverbed of the Black Umfolozi. Here, motionless, stood a black wildebeest (gnu). These comical ungulates are commonly seen in large herds on the African plains but to gaze on this solitary and awkward shape transported me into a dimension which conquered any remnant of the city life's burdens that might have arrived with me. The bondage of modern routine was liberated with an intensity of great magnitude. Again I renounced convention and allowed my imagination to take control.

Walking along the wooden path from my bamboo-thatched dwelling I reached the main boma (meeting place) of the lodge. I had only been there for five minutes when

99

an emerald-spotted wood dove flew into a closed window and fell to the ground. I ran to the little bird and picked her up gently. Her delicate neck was hanging limply as if disengaged from her body, and blood was seeping from her mouth. The impact had broken her neck. This was the perpetual legend of bush life, life and death which in itself effected a continuation of existence. With that, I looked up towards a scraping sound. It was two crowned hornbills excavating a tree trunk, indeed a well-chosen site for the imminent breeding and nesting season.

Later that night, whilst I was watching a blood red moon ascend over the ephemeral pools of the black Umfolozi, a slight breeze betrayed the distant high-pitched chorus of chuckling hyenas. This physically concealed expression of ancient Africa, unchanged since the beginning of time, aroused the spiritual yearning I had come to know so well. As the moon climbed, its radiance extinguished the glimmering Milky Way, but illuminated the riverbed with a haunting beam of light. As if by some obscure cue, and from the void of this vast wilderness, lions announced their approach. The distant whuffing communicated their positions, which completed the scenario of a perfect African night.

At 04.30hrs I rose to the sounds of an awakening land. In the chill of pre-dawn, lions roared again, seemingly closer this time. I sat on my veranda and surveyed the lightening sky. It was as if the moonrise of the evening before was being replayed. But this time around it wasn't the moon. It was the unhurried advancing of a rising sun. I had never before been witness to such replication.

Rest your spirit in her solitary places, for the gifts of life are the earth's, and they are given to all.

From Orion Rises on the Dune, The Outermost House
Henry Beston

100

FEBRUARY 1ST

2009

GIANT'S CASTLE,
UKHAHLAMBA DRAKENSBERG PARK

I DEPARTED FROM DURBAN IN THE RAIN. AFTER one and a half hours of driving I reached the rural township of Hlatikulu, modestly concealed in the foothills of the Giant's Castle range.

Clouds began changing place, and as I watched the castle of the legendary giant appear through the gaps thunder grumbled in the distance. The verdant velvety green of summer draped the approaching slopes.

It was early but already young boys had gathered together with their tall, skinny dogs. They all sat together in the dusty shade of a thorn tree and I wondered if they were about to herd their grazing stock elsewhere. Both boys and dogs looked contented; I smiled and waved. They waved back. To the left of this group was a youngster, probably around seven years of age, riding bareback on a whitish grey pony. Together they cantered through fields decorated with cosmos, a delicate yet flamboyant spread of pastel blooms, and their delight was tangible.

I had a flashback to my schooldays, those days when we as children ambled through the English countryside together. We would gently pluck flowers from the ground and then make daisy chains for the ones whom we loved.

Goats carefully crossed the road, whilst cows and sheep nibbled on grassless verges. Churchgoers in their full-length blue and white attire spoke of their faith, whilst courting couples giggled and teased each other. Young men standing on pedals steered their bicycles at breakneck speed through the dusty streets, whilst older men could be seen fixing old, well-used vehicles in the security of their yards.

As I neared the mountain camp a grey duiker darted across the road in front of me, probably to meet his mate on the other side. I reflected on all my twenty-first century

101

associates back home in the metropolis of Durban. They had warned me of all the dangers that I could encounter in isolated areas such as these!

I felt fortunate that I was able to discern Africa's ability to facilitate the need for some people to trace an existence of paradox; a paradox between medicinal balm for the soul and that of a potentially dangerous survival.

It is in the midst of these extremes that faith is truly born.

Quote:

Courage is the power to let go of the familiar.

Mary Bryant

FEBRUARY 2ND
2009

I ENJOYED BREAKFAST ON MY DECK. A RED-WINGED starling had joined me and was singing for his share. Today I decided to take the well-known track down to the Bushman River. A butterfly, elegantly dressed in orange and black, whispered past me and rested on a bough a little further on. I have a friend in England who, whenever visited by a butterfly, is aware, in her own mind, of her late husband's presence. I focused on the butterfly's markings, which imitated two large eyes. They seemed to be searching my essence.

I had a private conversation with this delicate being, and it then closed its wings as if in deep thought. I waited for some kind of response. After some time I spoke again. "Well, I can't wait all day, I must carry on." Before I moved a hair the butterfly flew ahead of me, as far as the river, the Bushman River; the river which, for me, will always link this world with the next.

Quote:

Happiness is like a butterfly, pursued it is always beyond your grasp, but sometimes if you sit quietly, it may come unexpectedly and alight upon you.

Nathaniel Hawthorne

April 27TH
2009

My 60TH Birthday!

THIS PRESENT TO MYSELF WAS THE FRUITION of an escape into the Namib Desert, a place I had dreamed of visiting for twenty-five years.

During the days of a 'thirtysomething' youngster I had visited Namibia (its name, in those days was South West Africa and it was embroiled in a guerrilla war against South Africa). My friend and I had travelled over eight thousand kilometres on gravel roads in the hope of discovering declining pockets of wilderness.

Now, having arrived in Namibia from Durban in South Africa I chartered a plane from the capital city Windhoek. I wanted to set eyes on the world's oldest sand dunes and to gaze upon Big Mama, its highest.

Soon after lift-off the pilot and I were far away from any signs of habitation. The little plane was unable to transcend the hot afternoon thermals which shook the single-engine Cessna, tossing it around as if it didn't matter. The tiny shadow of outstretched wings skimmed the knotted landscape and strange rock formations below us. I hadn't seen anything like this before. One hour into the flight outlying homesteads were no longer visible and then, like a mirage, the desert sand dunes emerged ahead of us. They were detectable as a hazy mist.

There was no sign of life. There was no water anywhere, just gravel roads criss-crossing each other. Where they were going, and where I was going, I couldn't imagine. Almost as if reading my thoughts the pilot turned to me and pointed out the airstrip on which we were to land. I honestly couldn't see it. Suddenly the plane made a sharp turn to the right, its wings in an almost vertical position. I closed my eyes, and left the rest to fate.

Following the few short kilometres to the lodge in a desert truck I was escorted to my little kulala (dwelling). Its outlook reached over desert grassland towards the ancient mountains and I could see the sand dunes in the distance, towards a western sky.

104

On the deck was a plunge pool in which I immediately spotted the limp body of a female sociable weaver. Sociable weavers, as their name implies, build their nests within a condominium-type establishment. Together, in unity, an enormous nest is built, often within the starkness of a dead tree. It was the only unhappy event of my sojourn in the desert.

As a surprise treat for me birthday celebrations took place that night. During dinner the staff sang and danced. Their ethnic custom was outspoken, their hospitality encapsulating, and their warmth pervaded the cold night air of the desert. Sirius spoke to me from the darkest sky I had ever gazed upon. I seemed to absorb the ancient wisdom descending to the desert floor on which I stood. I was mesmerised.

I pondered on the words of Credo Muthwa: *"Magic was the science of the ancient people."*

The crescent moon lay on its back, visible only for a short time before the earth turned and coaxed it on its way to another part of the globe. I knew that the light of the stars on which my eyes were set had left their origin many centuries ago. Knowing this, I felt able to connect with the generations of man and beast that had inhabited this earth of ours since time had begun. I felt small and inconspicuous as I became sentient of the frailty of a passing life. I was thankful for the choices that I had made in life and for my ability to empathise with cosmic creation. I recall praying to the universe. It was as if a tsunami of vibrations were seeking my soul. I let them in. I pleaded so hard for answers to the problems of this century; the cruelty to animals, inhumanity, the degradation of our planet. My entreaty was to find some small way in which I could help.

APRIL 28TH

2009

T HE JOURNEY FROM THE LODGE TO THE dunes took me over rough gravel tracks through desolate patches of desert concessions. It was cold, but the anticipation of arrival for sunrise stoked the glow within me. As we passed a lonely homestead a hot air balloon was preparing to ascend the gentle thermal currents. I took a moment to consider the authenticity of the sight on which I stared. It was 'out of this world'.

A little further on the vehicle came to a halt on a sandy elevation. As I gazed towards a deep orange glow in the eastern sky night switched abruptly into day. The mountain range revealed a dark red, crescent-shaped orb, silently greeting the starkness of this virtually lunar landscape. As the rising sun disclosed its light, as it had done every day since the beginning of time, the hot air balloon I had seen back on the plains rose in unison. The sand dunes which enveloped me absorbed the sun's rays and gradually illuminated colours such that I had never seen. The heavenly paintbrush smeared them in reds, browns, gold and ochre. The dune's grasses glistened in celebration. A gently humming breeze began to form ripples in the sand which stretched for miles. Evidence of desert creatures was apparent for anyone wishing to find it. Tiny footprints spoke softly of desert larks and barking geckos, uninterrupted as they went.

Total silence can be contemplated but rarely experienced. This oasis of desert simplicity becalmed silent moments such as I had never known. The extraterrestrial vista of the earth from a space shuttle would be, in my view, the only possible supersedence of this universal wonder.

Leaving this placid scene the sandy route led to both Dead Vlei and Sossusvlei, areas of world acclaim for their unique isolation, habitat and antiquity. The Atlantic Ocean was just twenty-three kilometres away, its western lip blocked by the mighty dunes. En route there were springbok in small numbers, a pair of jackal, and a few ostrich which dug furiously in the sand in search of anything edible. Amidst this unforgiving environment the sight which I had longed to glean, in almost picture book stance, was a gemsbok. This huge antelope was dwarfed by the mighty dunes behind him. I was in a state of complete awe.

Dead Vlei, as the name implies, revealed a dry clay pan which over time had expedited the death of the trees that had attempted to survive the parched conditions. To reach the vlei I had to scale an impressive sand dune of colossal proportion. I eventually reached the summit, having stumbled many times in the deep sand. The crest of the dune was narrow and concentration was required to maintain balance. I remembered I was now sixty years of age and felt pleased with my effort! A panoramic view beset me. A sea of sand for as far as the eye could see. Arid, forbidding sand dunes. It was obvious that so few living organisms could survive here.

April 30TH
2009

LETTER TO A FRIEND

I HAVE JUST BURIED A SOCIABLE WEAVER IN the sand just in front of my kulala. The male has been coming twice a day ever since I found his mate drowned in my plunge pool on the day of my arrival. I removed the weaver and lay her on top of the deck's log fencing. After I buried her I became witness to a strange phenomenon.

I dug a shallow grave in which I placed the little bird. I then covered the hole with a largish rock and made a crucifix from some twigs, onto which I tied some flowering grasses. No sooner had I climbed back onto my deck than a flock of sociable weavers flew onto the sand surrounding the grave. They pecked the sand and then in groups of four or five sat on the rock prior to flying off. I am, of course, loathe to be anthropomorphic, but the male hasn't been back since I buried his mate.

I have been sad and although I know that life and death are both part of the whole I was witness to the male sociable weaver's distress. However, apart from that, it is here where I have discovered a paradise lost in the desolation of Namibia.

The only sounds are those of the birds as they fly into the camp's small waterhole. Ruppell's korrhan, Namaqua sandgrouse and a pair of pale chanting goshawks. A falcon alights in a tree close by on occasions, threatening other birds who may need some liquid revival.

There is a contentment here that I simply cannot explain, but I sense it with a passionate deepness. There is a stillness and a sentiment of such generosity. It's as if it is gifted from the untamed natural world to the human tribe. How blessed are we who find it, are nourished by it, and who live our lives for it. How fortunate are those of us who do not have to explain it, define it or own proof of evidence for it. It is simply a tranquillity which strengthens and sustains us. Such personal liberation seeks out an intimacy which is difficult to replicate elsewhere.

MAY
2009

06.15HRS DURBAN

Driving to work on the road less travelled.
Every new bend in the road bestows its own delight.
Ahead of me, an elephant's trunk is reaching out to touch a dolphin's nose,
Whilst the fullness of an amber moon slides behind them in the sky.
Like all clouds, the theme imparts a reflection of the mind's eye.
An elephant from the African plains, and a dolphin from the secrecy of the sea
Join 'hands' in celestial jubilation. It's a visionary miracle.

JUNE

2009

GIANT'S CASTLE CAMP

A RETURN TO THE DRAKENSBERG MOUNTAINS DID NOT disappoint me. As always there was a generosity of passion and spirit which abounded in this foreboding cavern of ancient, pristine earthly space.

I was aware that the redemptive power of the landscape seeped into my inner being. The carved magnificence of peaks and valleys were the same as I always remembered them. The sandstone caves remained, continuing to peer down onto the chiselled floor of the valley. They established a supremacy over the twists and turns of the lively Bushman River.

But the Bushmen were gone. The Bushmen who were chased by the encroachment of advancing human races were absent. When they lived these small descendants of creation would have been occupied with the preparation of their quiver arrows. They then would have left the warmth of the fire in the cave, and after embracing their wives and children, set off to hunt. They would have vanished into the hostile isolation and harshness of the expedition. In the winter this would have taken place in the snowy reaches of the foothills and peaks. On many occasions this would have hidden all traces of animal spoor, so vital for successful tracking.

I could sense the "whoosh" of the arrow as it left the bushman's bow. I could hear the sudden bleating of the felled buck. I could imagine the chase that followed. I could picture the deft manner in which the dead buck would have been strapped to the back of the small Bushman prior to the long and difficult haul home, and back to the warmth and safety of the cave. I could perceive the return of cave unity.

The caves are empty now, except for inquisitive baboons, and the exquisitely painted interiors, inner sanctums which tell of the joys, the sorrows, the struggles and the dreams of a long forgotten and extinct race. It was impossible not to be moved as witness to these works of art, which depict events in the history of man.

Nevertheless, the mountains stand firm in their account of past trials and accomplishments. The Bushman River still flows, transmitting sensations of past times to all who wish to comprehend them.

In a way, I could relate this disappearance of species to the monkeys in the suburbs of our modern world. Today, these relations of ours have lost their habitat, which have subsequently evolved into urban sprawls. They are shot at, maimed by catapults and trapped in hideously cruel snares.

As I walked along the valley floor leading away from Giant's Castle Camp I entered the primordial interval of anticipated dawn. It was the stillness that I recall. The running waters of the Bushman River continued. The orange glow infiltrating the wintery night sky warmed my soul. The chilliness of pre-dawn ebbed away. Birdsong, the will to live, the outpouring of gratitude; it was all there.

Hidden away by the tall grasses and the large riverine boulders I was completely overwhelmed by the sight which met my eyes. Partially concealed by the secrecy of a rising mist stood an eland and her calf drinking from the life-giving water. On this bend of the Bushman River nothing much had changed.

July

2009

A TROOP OF VERVET MONKEYS HAVE JUST TRAVELLED through my garden. It is wintertime and it is very dry. It is a very real privilege to have these primates enter into a human's window of life. They were thirsty. Two adults with six babies, the latter no more than twenty centimetres in height. The adults jumped up onto the rim of the bird bath and demonstrated to their offspring what had to be done. Next came six little baby monkeys equidistant around the bird bath's rim. Some cupped their hands and filled them with water as they had been shown by the adults. The rest simply leaned forwards, and lowering their tiny faces into the water, began to drink.

Then, they were gone…

The Invitation
By Oriah Mountain Dreamer

It doesn't interest me what you do for a living.
I want to know what you ache for,
And if you dare to dream of meeting your heart's longing.

It doesn't interest me how old you are.
I want to know if you will risk looking like a fool for love;
for your dream; for the adventure of being alive.

It doesn't interest me what planets are squaring your moon…
I want to know if you have touched the centre of your own sorrow, if you have been
opened by life's betrayals or have become shrivelled and closed from fear of further
pain.

I want to know if you can sit with pain,
mine or your own, without moving to hide it or fade it or fix it.

I want to know if you can be with joy,
mine or your own, if you can dance with wildness,
and let the ecstasy fill you to the tips of your fingers and toes without cautioning us to
be careful,
to be realistic or to remember the limitations of being human.

It doesn't interest me if the story you are telling me is true.
I want to know if you can disappoint another to be true to yourself.
If you can bear the accusation of betrayal and not betray your own soul.
If you can be faithless and therefore trustworthy.

I want to know if you can see beauty even when it is not pretty every day.
And if you can source your own life from its presence.

I want to know if you can live with failure, yours and mine, and still stand at the edge
of the lake and shout to the silver of the moon, "yes."

It doesn't interest me to know where you live, or how much money you have.
I want to know if you can get up after the night of grief and despair,
weary and bruised to the bone, and do what needs to be done to feed the children.

It doesn't interest me who you know or how you came to be here.
I want to know if you will stand in the centre of the fire with me and not shrink back.

It doesn't interest me where or what or with whom you have studied.

I want to know what sustains you from the inside when all else falls away.
I want to know if you can be alone with yourself and if you truly like the company you
keep in the empty moments.

I read this beautiful poem in the St Augustine's hospital magazine following its application during a team building exercise in 2009.

I felt an irrepressible inclination to respond.

My reply to 'The Invitation of Oriah Mountain Dreamer'

Indeed Oriah, I can be myself, can you?
I am a tourist, and I ache to find out how it was before we lost ourselves in the
suburbs. I dare to dream that I can meet people who still own their lives.

I am old enough, but in essence live some of my life vicariously through the younger
generation.
I have risked looking like a fool for love, and for my dreams,
but isn't that the adventure of which you speak, the adventure of an eternal journey?

I want you to know I am guided by Sirius and Orion. Taurus and Leo speak to me.
Yes, Oriah, sorrow I have known well,
and betrayals have played their part.
each time however, it seems I am better for it.

I can sit with pain, be it mine or another's,
and yes I can dance with the wildness of a lioness,
symbolising her courage, love and divinity. I try to play my part.

To truly love life is to cast out inhibitions, it must not however,
be at the expense of any other mortal.

It is impossible to be true to oneself, if one is not true to others.
I have both shed and drunk from the crucible of disappointment.
It is my faith which has created my trustworthiness.
How can I be faithless?

Every day I am thankful for all the joy I have known,
for all the people whom I have met and for all the animals that I have loved.
I live in hope that others may have found comfort from glancing through the window
of my soul.

Around which lake is it that you wish to dance and shout about failure?
I will gladly walk with you and sing loudly about my own.

I live close by.
Close enough to see the pain and despair of which you speak.
I have enough money for the things I need.

I make no secret of those whom I know,
or of how I came to be here.
It is what I have done with my apportioned talents that may help me gain entry into
the big mountain in the sky.
Do you think we will make it?
I would never leave you in a circle of fire.

It is so long ago, that even I can't remember where,
what or with whom I studied.
You will just have to trust me Oriah. I don't think it really matters.
You ask what sustains me from the inside when all else falls away.
I will confide in you in part.

It is to be in nature's wild places where I can be alone with myself, and to truly like
the company I keep in the empty moments.
It is especially in the mountains,
where I can sense how alone the Bushman must have felt on his hunt.
But lonely? Oh no, Oriah.
The earth's riches surrounded him,
and his gatherers eagerly awaited his return.

It has been an experience of great humility responding to your invitation,
and it is with heartfelt anticipation that I meet with your approval.

Ibubhezi.
Lioness of the Wilderness

JULY 25TH

2009

IN MY GARDEN AT HOME

Quote:

Travel is like a book, to read one page does not tell the story

Saint Augustine

THIS IS MY LAST ENTRY IN MY journal.

Two purple-crested loeries have come to visit and they are bouncing through the branches of the leopard tree. Two black-collared barbets are bombarding them as they are preparing a nest for their young. The loeries remain steadfast in their purpose. I like to think that they have come to wish me luck and to give thanks for the attempt to ignite that spark in someone else's soul.

It's a relay really, isn't it? An aspiration that the baton will continue to be passed on.

The earth is not something to be exploited and manipulated for our own greedy needs. It is an inheritance, worthy of handing over to the next generations of all living species.

For we truly are the guardians of this mystical place.

THREE MIRACLES

In March 2009, I received something from England in my post box. As was usual, on returning home from a long day at work, I stopped the car at the bottom of the driveway and collected the mail. I threw the couple of letters onto the dining room table, and went about my usual routine, leaving the mail unopened.

Later that evening I sat down to read my letters. Nothing, and I mean nothing, could have prepared me for what I was about to read. To celebrate the UK Born Free Foundation's twenty-fifth anniversary Virginia McKenna was to be hosting a safari to East Africa in October 2009. This was to be a specialist safari, the focus being a return to Kenya. I had been invited!

The safari promised to visit Meru National Park, the land of Elsa's birth and of her rehabilitation. It was also where the cheetah, Pippa, had been released back into the wild from her captive environment. Shaba Reserve appeared on the itinerary, a beautifully remote area where Joy Adamson was murdered whilst she was writing a book about her most recent work with Penny, a leopard.

I continued to read. I was having trouble focusing. I felt as though I was being transported into a realm that only a few would encounter.

Kenya in 2003 was, for me, my 'once in a lifetime miracle'. Elsa the lioness had facilitated my deeply meaningful journey. I had emerged from Meru, affected by a force that I was unable to fully explain. It had proven to be, in every possible sense of the concept, *a thin place.* Thin places are said to be close to divinity due to their beauty or serenity.

Not many people come to realise more than one miracle in their lifetime. Nevertheless, my second miracle was spending time with Virginia in her English home, an enchanting retreat in Surrey, not only charmed by the lives of her beloved family, but also a home adorned with African memories. Perhaps I had been seated in a chair in which George Adamson had chosen to sit when he spent time there. I found Virginia to be a truly gracious lady, in whose company I felt exquisitely at ease. We talked and I was quick to realise, in the words of JRR Tolkien, "*Not all those who wander are lost.*" I felt refreshingly reassured that those who seek understanding, from a transcendental perspective, become kindred spirits with similarly minded people.

This in part clarified as to why places become so important in the lives of those who search. Answers to questions are sought, and these answers appear to come from the universe.

The letter on my dining room table was the third and the most valuable miracle. Little Elsa's collar would now be buried in Meru.

MARIE

THE LAST PICTURE THAT I TOOK of Marie was just one day before I sent off my final additions for the book to Melrose Books in England. It was all very uncanny really, and it was as if Marie and I subconsciously knew she was going to leave this earth.

On Monday July 27th 2009 I took one day's annual leave from work, something I don't ever remember doing before.

I suggested that we take a drive to Weenen Game Reserve, a two hour drive away from Durban. We had never been there before but we knew it to be a place of great tranquillity and beauty. We packed a picnic and set off. Marie had requested that I take with me the last additions I had made for my book *Excerpts from an African Diary*. After seeing a good deal of game, and passing only one other vehicle, we came across an idyllic spot. It was totally secluded, and a little path led to an escarpment edge. The view was spectacular. There, far below us was the Bushman River, which appeared as a thin strip of winding ribbon. In front of us was, as Cecil Rhodes put it, "Miles and miles of bloody Africa."

We ate, and drank a glass of wine. I read to Marie the last pieces of the book which she had not yet read herself.

I am left wondering. Just what was going through Marie's mind when I snapped the last photograph that I was ever to take of my African friend? Marie was admitted to hospital on the night of July 31st. She died on August 9th 2009, a public holiday in South Africa. The day remembers great women, and is called Women's Day.

Ancient legend of the circle of friends

Ancient legend says that at the end of the evening friends would gather around a fire and share their hearts. They would speak of the good qualities of each other and remember times shared. As the embers faded, friendship was said to be sealed anew, bringing them closer together.

September 27TH

2009

WEENEN GAME RESERVE

TODAY I PLACED SOME OF MARIE'S ASHES on the gentle breeze, which tenderly carried them down to the floor of the valley, through which the Bushman River flows.

It has been exactly two months since Marie sat on this secluded site and pondered, as she gazed over the daunting abyss.

Three of us now spoke in turns into the aching void, as the remnants of Marie's mortal existence found their space and blended with Eternity.

The ancients knew something we seem to have forgotten.

Albert Einstein

Dust in the air suspended, marks the place where the story ended.

T.S.Eliot

Biography

Born in 1949 and raised in England.

The most profound influence in my life was the story of Joy and George Adamson and the lioness, Elsa. This was captured so movingly in the film *Born Free*. This story continued to influence my thinking, not only regarding the freedom of wild animals, but about the spiritual connection between humans and animals.

My nursing training in London exposed me to further experiences of the physical and spiritual needs of people and by the end of 1970 I knew that my life would be different. I needed a meaningful relationship with our planet.

I first met Africa in 1972, en route to New Zealand. I was never the same again. During the years I spent in New Zealand, I became acquainted with solace, hiking mountain passes and through wild places. It was easy to perceive God here, and I subsequently converted to Catholicism

In 1988, following extensive travel in southern Africa, I made my home there. Travelling continued as did my spiritual wealth. I journeyed to Kenya, and visited Elsa the lioness's grave and thereafter I contacted Virginia McKenna and we became friends

Africa and those akin to it are different